LIVING WITH A
DRINKER

How to change things

Mary Wilson
in Association with the Scottish Council
on Alcohol

Thorsons
An Imprint of HarperCollinsPublishers

Thorsons
An Imprint of HarperCollins*Publishers*
77–85 Fulham Palace Road,
Hammersmith, London W6 8JB
1160 Battery Street,
San Francisco, California 94111–1213

First published by Pandora 1989
This edition 1994
1 3 5 7 9 10 8 6 4 2

A catalogue record for this book
is available from the British Library

ISBN 0 7225 3038 2

Printed in Great Britain by
HarperCollinsManufacturing Glasgow

CONTENTS

Preface   vii

Introduction: Is this book for you?   1

1: Making sense of how you feel   7
   Anxiety   8
   Feeling useless   10
   Anger, frustration and resentment   15

2: All about alcohol   20
   Alcohol, the drug   21
   Alcohol and your body   21
   Alcohol and your behaviour   23
   Measuring how much you drink   24
   What is safe drinking?   28
   Your own drinking   30
   What do you know about alcohol?   31

3: Your partner and alcohol   34
   What kinds of people drink too much?   34
   Facts about problem drinkers   35
   How much does your partner drink?   37
   How does your partner use alcohol?   38
   Problems that drinking can cause   39

Does your partner need help? 42

4: Coping with drinking 44
Trying to survive the effects 45
Why drinkers often deny the problem 46
How do you cope? 48
How *should* you react? 50
Taking action on drinking: a personal contract 63
If your partner decides to do something about
  drinking 66
Hopes and disappointments 72

5: Coping with life 74
Unhelpful changes 75
Being good to yourself 77
Learning what is best for yourself 107
Making plans for the future 118

6: Your children 125
What children need 127
Your own children 128
Preparing children for emergencies 130
Guidelines for children 134

7: Taking stock 139
Have things changed? 140
Coping with difficulties 142
Your future with your partner 145

Useful addresses 155
Further reading 163
Index 165

PREFACE

This book is for the many people who cannot cope with their partner's drinking problem. It is designed to help people understand the problems caused by alcohol, to guide readers to discover their own solutions to these problems in the light of their own feelings and needs, and to rebuild the confidence required to carry their decisions through.

Living With a Drinker arose out of my training work with the Scottish Council on Alcohol (SCA), and most particularly out of the workshops that focused on working with partners. The inspiration came from my colleague, John Cuthbert, Manager of the Glasgow Council on Alcohol where I worked as a counsellor. He, Pat Baillie of the Alcohol Studies Centre, Ann Lancaster of the SCA, and I formed a working group in 1985 to analyse and draw up the objectives, structure, and content of the book. *Living With A Drinker* is the amended published version of our pilot self-help book. I am grateful to all the members of the group for their support, constructive criticism and imaginative ideas.

I want to extend warm thanks to Ian Robertson for his invaluable, detailed comments about the content and presentation of our pilot version, and to Margaret Stevenson for encouraging me to seek a publisher for the book. Candida Lacey, my commisioning editor, has been a source of encouragement, advice and moral support throughout the project, and I am particularly grateful for her continuing loyalty during a difficult period of my own ill health. Linda Cusick and Anna Black provided their clerical support in a generous, efficient, and very friendly way.

I would finally like to thank Mary Bradley and all the other counsellors and clients whose experiences and ideas gave me the motivation to write this book.

Mary F. Wilson

INTRODUCTION: IS THIS BOOK FOR YOU?

This book is written for the *other* people in a drinker's life, in the understanding that they can be hurt as much, if not more, by the problems caused by drinking. Although relatives and friends of the drinker should all find the book helpful, it is aimed especially at *partners*.

Many partners of problem drinkers suffer from guilt, isolation, loneliness, fear, anger and a sense of helplessness. They desperately want to influence the drinking but often fail. They may be worried about the risk of abuse to themselves and their children, and how to cope with financial and legal problems.

If you are seriously affected by someone's drinking, this book is designed to help you cope with the problems that you face. It gives advice on influencing the drinking, but more importantly it will help you to make changes which will give you more control over your *own* life.

KAREN:

I was always aware that Roddy was quite a heavy drinker – even before we got married. But he always seemed to be able to hold his drink, and it wasn't until after the baby was born that I began to notice problems. He never seemed to be at home, and when he was he was either just asleep in a chair or just going on at me about showing no interest in him.

Now I'm only working part-time, I can see that a lot of money is being spent on drinking. I've also heard from a neighbour that Roddy's being pulled up at work for drinking too much at lunchtime. I wouldn't say Roddy's an alcoholic, by any means, but his drinking is definitely beginning to spoil our family life and I'm starting to panic about how I'll cope if things get a lot worse.

Most partners of problem drinkers are women, but this book will be helpful to *anyone* who is seriously affected by someone else's drinking pattern.

PARTNERS OF PROBLEM DRINKERS

You have probably picked up this book because you are concerned about the heavy drinking of someone close to you. Maybe you are afraid, or convinced, that drinking is hurting this person and others as well. Your greatest hope may be to persuade your partner to cut down or to stop drinking permanently. You may feel helpless because your efforts so far have failed. Perhaps you feel that your partner doesn't care for you since he or she won't cut down or quit. You may feel guilty, and even blame yourself for the drinking – your partner may even be blaming you.

But you *can* change things and this book can help you to do so: first, by helping you to understand what has been happening to you, and second, by helping you to gain greater control over your own life. You may find that your partner is able to change as well. But even if that fails to happen, life can get better for you. You, too, have a right to happiness.

Right now, however, you are probably feeling pretty miserable. For example:

Guilt: Perhaps you feel guilty due to misplaced loyalty. You may even feel guilty about reading a book like this one, or about seeking professional advice. Many drinkers lay blame for their behaviour at the door of those closest to them. You may even have come to believe some of the accusations. But it is unlikely to be your fault.

Loneliness: When there is a drinker in the family many people stay away from friends, relations and neighbours, thereby increasing their loneliness. This book will help to show you how to avoid being lonely.

Fear: Anxiety is natural when you're worrying about what might happen next, wondering how on earth you'll cope. But these fears can be resolved.

Helplessness: You may have been told that nothing can be done until the drinker is 'ready' to do something for himself. Please don't believe this. A great deal can be done for you and for the drinker.

Anger: Anger is common and often justified. This book will help you to cope with it and to use it in constructive ways.

Abuse: Sadly, abuse is very common. It may be of a verbal nature, with your partner ridiculing, humiliating or threatening you. It may involve physical attacks or unwanted sexual demands. Far more help is available now than ever before, and women have legal rights as far as housing, legal, and financial problems are concerned. See pages 120 and 159 for information on these and other practical problems.

Depression: All these problems can spiral down into depression. You can be left feeling worthless, unlovable, and unable to make any changes. But you have already taken the first step in starting to read this book. If what you've read so far makes sense in terms of what is going on around you, then the book should help you.

Stewart's life changed radically after his little boy was killed in an accident and his wife June became a heavy drinker. Stewart was looking after his son at the time, and has always blamed himself for the boy's death. He also feels responsible for June's drinking and takes sleeping pills every night because he is very depressed.

Last weekend my sister came to visit, and suddenly started talking to me about June's drinking. I've been so ashamed I've never talked to anyone about it before, nor tried to do anything about it or even understand it. But all the time I've been feeling guilty, tired, depressed and trapped. My sister made me realise I shouldn't give up, that I had to keep my own life going, and that there must be some things I could do to try and make things better for both of us. It won't be easy, but I can see I'll have to make a start somewhere.

HOW TO USE THE BOOK

This book tries to cover everything that partners of problem drinkers have to cope with but some parts of the book will be more useful to you than others. You can see from the table of contents which chapters are most relevant for you. It will also help you to refer back later to worksheets and other entries you want to reread. You might want to start with a section that especially concerns you. If you feel, for example, that there is a danger of you and your children being harmed by your partner, turn straight to the section about preparing children for emergencies (pages 130–2). If you are uncertain about whether or not alcohol is the real cause of the problems in your relationship, it is worthwhile reading Chapter 3 first.

Every chapter ends with a summary of the main points. The book has been designed to help you understand and tackle your specific problems. Parts of the book are designed specially for you to write in. It is important to resist the temptation of skipping these exercises. They will help you reach your own decisions about how you want to improve your life.

Many of the problems you are likely to face are illustrated by case histories. These cases are based on real difficulties which people have brought to alcohol counsellors, but the people and situations have been altered to ensure their privacy. Not all of them will be relevant to your situation, and they are less important than the exercises which are vital and relevant to everyone concerned about drinking.

Try working from the book in a quiet moment each day. Don't read too much at once. If you have a lot of problems try to be patient and realistic about them.

And please don't feel that because this is a self-help guide it means you must cope with everything alone. Make use of support groups and other people, organisations, professionals, anyone you feel can help you. The book should help you to regain lost confidence in yourself and a belief in your own ability to change things for the better. I sincerely hope it will.

1

MAKING SENSE OF HOW YOU FEEL

If you live with your partner you are bound to have very strong feelings about his or her drinking. If you've come to trust and depend on your partner, and you've been together a long time, then your feelings of hurt and betrayal will be strong. But it may be that you don't live with your partner, or that you are reading this book because you're worried about a relative or friend. Then you may be in a better position to distance yourself from the drinker's problems.

This chapter will help you to understand and deal with the feelings described on pages 3–4. It should help you feel calmer and leave you less confused, with more time and energy for other things. Freeing yourself from bad feelings should pave the way towards making the important changes discussed in Chapter 5, 'Coping with Life'.

If you are close to the problem drinker, you may

well feel upset. A great deal is happening to trouble you and feeling bad can become a way of life. You learn not to expect very much pleasure or happiness. Instead, all you can think about is avoiding or escaping further trouble and upset. Emotions change from *anxiety* to *anger*, and to feelings of *helplessness* and *worthlessness*.

Cathie lives around the corner from her mother. She knows her mother has been drinking heavily since her father died nine months ago, and also taking pills from the doctor for her 'nerves'. Three months ago her mother broke her arm in a fall, and the break isn't mending well.

I'm so worried about Mum. I call in three times a day. This isn't easy, because I've got three small children to look after. I cook her meals, but she hardly touches them. She always insists she only drinks a little, and won't talk to her doctor about her drinking. I feel completely helpless, but just can't get Mum out of my mind. I've lost interest in the things I used to do, and now my husband Stan is getting angry because I spend so much time at Mum's. My nerves are so bad I'm tempted to ask my doctor if he'll give me some more pills too.

ANXIETY

Feeling unable to change things you are forced to live with can cause constant worry and anxiety. The behaviour of your partner, or, in Cathie's case, her mother, may cause additional uncertainty and confusion as he or she becomes more and more unpredictable. When you go out, you worry about what you may come back to. When your partner goes out you fear for the worst when he or she returns: a family row, or a physical injury to someone if there has been a history of abuse.

Doubts about yourself may cause anxiety, too. You may not know how to cope with the drinking since if you challenge it you could set off a fight. Often you may find yourself doing just the reverse of what you mean to do. For example, you might decide to go to a friend's house if your partner comes home drunk, but stay at home instead and end up rowing, while your partner places the blame for his or her drinking on your attitude. Then you may feel guilty, wondering if your shortcomings are somehow to blame. And this may spill over into the feeling of being 'no good as a parent', or imagining that your family and the neighbours see you as a 'problem family'.

Anxiety builds up for the partners of problem drinkers because of the uncertainties involved in living with a drinker. It builds up through trying to predict and control the behaviour of a drinker in hopes of protecting him from himself. You cannot control a drinker, but the desire to *try* to do so can become obsessive.

Anxiety is not caused just by what is going on around you. It is also produced by your thoughts and feelings about whatever is happening to you or by your having *unrealistic* expectations of yourself. You may be expecting things of yourself that no one can reasonably expect, and you may criticise yourself constantly for not achieving the impossible.

Anxiety can be lessened if you *learn how to tackle problems*, *think positively* about your life and *learn to relax*. By learning to deal with the practical problems caused by drinking, like debt and legal problems, you begin to feel in control of things. Making a telephone call to get help is a good way to start and you will find some useful addresses at the back of this book, on pages 155–61. Learning how to solve problems, how to think positively, and how to relax are all discussed in Chapter 5.

Margaret was very scared when she discovered three final notices for household bills in the post. They arrived after her husband Sam had gone to work. She had never dealt with money before, and was nervous about 'officialdom', but she knew from a friend that a Citizens Advice Bureau can be helpful about these matters.

> I plucked up courage to go but felt very panicky while I was on the bus, and wanted to turn back. Yet the man in the Bureau was very helpful. He worked out a really good way of paying off the debts which would still leave money in my pocket. He also talked about possible ways of making sure that a fixed amount from Sam's wages went towards paying bills in the future. I knew I would be welcome any time to get help with any extra problems.

FEELING USELESS

People trapped in a relationship which has been spoiled by drinking often end up underrating themselves. They constantly put themselves down. They feel that they have nothing to offer anyone, that they have no abilities or talents. Because they doubt themselves and are unable to change their lives they are plagued by feelings of helplessness. If you experience a sense of worthlessness, consider whether it is caused by:

- Your thoughts about the drinking
- The way the drinker acts towards you
- The way you are living now
- A combination of these things

Your thoughts about the drinking

For many partners, certain thoughts occur over and over again:

- There must be something wrong with me to have married an alcoholic.
- If I'd been a better wife to him he wouldn't have turned to drinking in the first place.
- I can't be worth caring about if she won't change her drinking for me.
- If I wasn't such a dead loss I'd be able to make her change.

Do your thoughts run along these lines? The fact is that people rarely end up abusing alcohol as a direct result of their relationships. These days, most young people drink a fair amount, and many drink heavily, so it is less likely that their drinking is seen as 'abnormal' by their partners and close friends.

Don't blame yourself and feel guilty about your partner's drinking. Your partner is an adult, responsible for him or herself. Get help by all means, but do not shoulder the blame and forget your own needs.

The way the drinker acts towards you

You may have started to think badly about yourself because of the way your partner has been behaving towards you. He or she, for example, may say or do things which give you a very poor view of yourself: agreeing to drink less on condition that you stop nagging, pay more attention to how you look, take more interest in his or her work problems, and so on.

Some drinkers seem to take every opportunity to put their partners down. They frown on or laugh at their partners' ideas and continually indicate that nothing that their partner does is good enough. Many problem drinkers are caring and loving people for *some* of the time, but if you are criticised *most* of the time you stop believing in yourself. The drinker's behaviour is often motivated by fear – he or she is afraid to value your opinions because they challenge excessive drinking. Even so, no attempt to hurt you should be tolerated: verbal attacks meant to make you feel wretched, or physical violence. If these are happening to you, turn to page 161 for possible sources of help.

Ian feels negative about himself because he lost a promotion two years ago, and because he is not a great success at socialising, whereas his girlfriend, with whom he lives, is a live-wire. He once found this very attractive, but feels that she is drinking too much now.

When we're out with friends and drinking she makes snide remarks about me. It used to be about just small things, and it was always said as a kind of joke. But now she gets really sarcastic about my lack of success at work, and has even 'made noises' about how I'm no good in bed. I feel all this anger boiling up inside me, but I don't want to have a row in front of friends.

The way you're living now

Feelings of well-being and self-esteem are tied up with feelings of achievement and image; we need to know we can make a go of things and are well thought of by the people we know and care for. So if your partner's drinking has caused you to lose touch with people and things you used to enjoy, you are jeopardising your own well-being.

Sometimes it is hard to keep going on as normal. Embarrassing and difficult things happen. It seems simpler to drift away from people. If you have children, they may shy away from bringing friends home and from outings with the drinker. You may have neglected your friends and your interests out of fear at leaving the drinker alone or with the children. This may have led you to become little more than a 'domestic caretaker', with more time to worry about the drinking problem and to doubt that you can cope.

One important point to remember is that you need to be good to yourself (see Chapter 5). If you want to cope, and to become strong enough to tackle the drinking, you need to spend time on yourself. This means working hard to build up your own confidence, staying in touch with people, doing things which make you feel better about yourself.

ALLISON:

I can see that as Eddie's drinking has increased

over the years, the things we used to do together don't interest him any more unless there's drink available. I've made the decision though that *I'm* still going to keep these interests going. I've always led a very active life, and though I'm worried about Eddie's drinking, I'm not going to stay at home fretting about it. I know it means we don't spend as much time together, but it seems very important that I don't allow my own life to be governed by Eddie's drinking.

You can make a start at tackling negative thoughts by working on the lists that follow. On the left-hand side of the page is a list of 'Negative thoughts': *unrealistic, unhelpful*, and *harmful* ways of thinking about oneself. These are the kinds of thoughts that lead to feelings of anxiety, worthlessness and depression. The list on the right-hand side contains 'Positive thoughts' which can help to keep things in perspective despite your partner's drinking. The idea is to cross off those items on the left which *don't* apply and to tick those on the right that *do* apply. Then, to concentrate on eliminating other negative thoughts from your life and on adding positive ones, by changing your thinking over the next few weeks.

Keep going back to the list to decide which 'Thoughts' to work on next. Add other thoughts to the list which apply specifically to your situation.

Negative thoughts	Positive thoughts
● If only I could stop doing . . .	● There are things I can do to make life better for myself.
● I wish I could be more like . . .	● Today I was able to . . .

- People really must think I'm stupid.

- No one else would have ended up in such a mess.

- I used to be able to cope far better than this.

- I always seem to make a mess of things.

- No one would be interested in someone like me.

- I never seem to be able to . . .

- I can't be worth caring about.

- There's nothing I can do to change things.

- Tomorrow I am going to try to . . .

- I have no more faults than the average person.

- One thing I have always been able to do well is . . .

- The last time something really bad happened, I managed to come through it OK.

- . . . still seem to enjoy my own company.

- I can manage as well as most people.

- I am not personally responsible for the fact that my partner drinks too much.

- I might feel better if I try . . .

ANGER, FRUSTRATION AND RESENTMENT

In a sense, feeling angry, frustrated and resentful is a better way of coping with being hurt than feeling anxious, helpless and worthless. You are at least feeling you don't deserve what is happening to you, and are more likely to consider taking some action. But you should aim to take action which is *positive* and which *pays off*. Simply getting rid of pent-up feelings can be unhelpful to you and your partner.

John is a headmaster whose son Robert is unemployed. Robert drinks heavily at weekends, with little of his unemployment pay-out left over for the family purse.

> I've tried everything I can think of to get Robert to sort out his drinking, including threatening to throw him out, and pleading with him to go to AA (Alcoholics Anonymous). Every weekend there's an awful showdown. I'm not prepared to become a 'client' by seeing a social worker or a counsellor. I'd be too embarrassed and ashamed – everyone like that knows me through my work. The fact that I can't control my own son, including getting him to find a job, has destroyed my confidence in myself. I feel both angry and helpless and all the worry involved is affecting my work.

You may feel that everyone else but you gets the lucky breaks in life, and that in spite of all your efforts everything goes against you. Luck *can* play a part in peoples' futures. But we all have to learn sooner or later how to plan and make changes for ourselves.

Getting what you deserve from other people means trying to hold back your feelings of frustration and resentment, and stating what you want in an assertive but kindly way. Attacking that person, showing them up in public or suggesting we have no faith in them gets their backs up and makes them want to do anything *but* help you.

If you can try to behave towards other people in a

way which shows that it is something that they *did*, rather than what they are, that you're unhappy with, they may feel more like listening. Coping in this way can be easier if you let your anger calm down a little before doing anything.

Remember that:

● Feeling angry is natural and normal
● Taking action can be helpful

But – it is important to:

● Put off what you want to do until you've cooled down.
● Be firm and if necessary repeat what you plan to do, but *not* in an angry way.
● Avoid attacking the person who has upset you – go for what it was that they *did* that upset you.

BE SURE YOU WERE RIGHT TO BE ANGRY IN THE FIRST PLACE

SUMMARY

Feeling anxious, angry and bad about yourself are all typical reactions to someone else's problem drinking. It would be strange if you did not to feel this way some of the time. Although these feelings are a result of the drinking problem, your own way of coping and your thoughts also have a part to play. It is important to believe that changing how you see and think about things can make you *feel* better about them.

Some people who are trapped with a drinker suffer crippling anxiety and/or deep-seated depression. If you are very depressed you may lose your appetite, have problems sleeping, find it difficult to concentrate and feel unable to get any pleasure out of life.

If you recognise these symptoms in yourself, you should see your doctor. Three excellent books on dealing with depression are listed on page 162. There are also some helpful hints on coping with depression on page 95, and with anxiety on page 102.

Meanwhile, you can start working on bad feelings by promising yourself, on the basis of what you've just read, to do any three things which you feel will help you to feel better. For example, you might decide to write a list of all the things you've done that you feel proud about. Write them down on the worksheet below.

There are suggestions for doing further work on the kinds of problems tackled here in Chapter 5.

ACTIVITY LIST

I promise to try these three things to help me to feel better.

1. ....
....
....
....

2. ....
....
....
....

3. ....
....
....
....

2

ALL ABOUT ALCOHOL

Your partner may claim to be an expert on alcohol, insisting you know nothing about it if you raise the subject. Or he may say 'If drinking is so bad, why do *you* drink?' Some partners may claim to drink no more than anyone else, or say that alcohol is not a serious risk to their health, or that spirits are stronger than beer. Perhaps he or she insists that drinking helps people calm their nerves or cope with depression. Eventually you may begin to feel that the problems you thought were caused through drinking are somehow separate from them.

The aim of this chapter is to help *you* to become the expert. It should help you to be quite clear about the effect alcohol has on people, and how people *should* drink if they want to avoid problems. If you drink, then this concerns you as well as your partner, but the information provided here is mainly to increase your expertise and confidence in assessing drinking problems.

ALCOHOL, THE DRUG

Most people enjoy having a drink with friends. It makes them feel more relaxed and sociable. In the West we've become so used to drinking alcohol socially that we forget that alcohol is a drug. In fact, alcohol is a *depressant*, slowing the system down rather than perking it up. It is a powerful drug that distorts emotions and changes behaviour. Alcohol is the cause of more accidents, violence, injury and crime than any other hard drug.

Although alcohol is full of calories (there are almost 200 calories in a pint of beer) it has no food value at all, and no vitamins or nutrients. Too much alcohol, moreover, can prevent absorption of the vitamins that are present in the food we eat.

Alcohol does not warm you up. On the contrary, alcohol reduces body temperature and should never be given to anyone suffering from the cold.

Finally, it is extremely dangerous to take drink and drugs together. Never mix the two. Taken with aspirin, alcohol irritates the stomach and can cause stomach ulcers. Prescribed drugs, like sedatives and tranquillisers, should never be combined with alcohol since at the very least they will cause drowsiness. Sleeping pills mixed with alcohol often has fatal results. Also, you should try to avoid mixing alcohol with pain killers and non-prescription cold cures.

ALCOHOL AND YOUR BODY

The human body works like a chemical factory, changing food and drink into substances useful for growth, health and energy. A natural chemical, alcohol does not need to be digested. It enters the bloodstream instantly and reaches the brain within minutes.

Those parts of the brain which deal with self-control and emotions are the first to be slowed down by alcohol, so that we relax, become chatty, and more sociable. But if we go on drinking, other parts of the brain also slow down. Making decisions becomes difficult, we slur words, and lose motor control, staggering, falling down, and even passing out. Drinking a large amount of alcohol very quickly can seriously slow down the heart-rate and breathing which in turn can lead to coma and even death.

Elizabeth's boyfriend doesn't drink a lot. When they drink on their own he merely becomes more talkative and affectionate, as well as obviously 'tiddly', but when they drink with friends it's an entirely different scenario.

Colin doesn't have to drink a lot to get really tipsy. Then he just goes downhill, talking a lot of gibberish, and sometimes bringing personal things into the conversation I'd rather not talk about. He also gets clumsy, and usually ends up bumping into things and people, and knocking a glass or two off the table. Then the next morning he can't remember a thing, although he always insists he didn't drink more than anyone else.

Our body gets rid of all the alcohol in our bloodstream by burning it up in the liver. This is why the liver can get damaged if we drink too much. Drinking black coffee, having a shower or taking exercise do not make the liver work any faster, so there is no 'quick' way to sober up. It takes your body about two hours to get rid of one pint of beer or one double whisky.

ALCOHOL AND YOUR BEHAVIOUR

Different people will be affected by alcohol in different ways. Some become silly, others aggressive. It often depends on how people feel when they begin to drink.

Larger and heavier people are usually affected less by the same amount of drink. The larger the person, the larger the bloodstream, and the more room there is for the alcohol.

People who drink regularly will seem to hold their drink better because the body has learned to 'tolerate' alcohol. Tolerance is a bad sign, not a good one.

Eating food before and while you are drinking can lessen the effects to some extent, as can drinking slowly and over a longer period of time. Although mixing spirits with fizzy drinks speeds up the rate at which alcohol gets into the system, drinking spirits undiluted is bad for the gullet and the stomach lining. *Drinking beer is just as dangerous as drinking spirits.*

Allison is the singer with a local jazz band. She has been living with Eddie, the bass player, for seven years.

Eddie has always combined drinking and music. During one music session he'll get through about four cans, but then he might go on and have a couple of 'super lagers'. I read a leaflet which showed this was the same as drinking half a bottle of gin. He refused to believe this, just saying he'd always enjoyed a few cans with the band, and wasn't going to stop now. But he's put on a lot of weight, although he hasn't much of an appetite.

MEASURING HOW MUCH YOU DRINK

You and your partner may have argued about the amount you both drink, what is an acceptable amount to drink, and when it is wise to call a halt. So how do you measure how much your partner drinks and how much you drink. And how much is too much?

There are two ways of measuring drinking. One is to measure the alcohol in the glass and the other is to measure the alcohol in the bloodstream.

Alcohol in the glass

Different drinks contain different strengths of alcohol and are served in different measures. However, the amount of alcohol in all the drinks in the diagram below is the *same*, and is measured as one unit of alcohol (sometimes called a 'standard unit' or 'standard drink').

ONE UNIT OF ALCOHOL equals 8–10 grams of pure alcohol. This means:-	**OR** a glass of fortified wine, sherry or port
½ pint of beer	
OR a glass of table wine	**OR** one single whisky

These units are based on normal pub or bar measures, not on measures poured at home which are usually much larger. There will be slight differences in pub or bar measures depending on the country in which you live.

HOW MANY UNITS IN YOUR DRINK?

Drink	Units
1 pub measure of spirits (whisky, gin, vodka)	1
1 glass of fortified wine (sherry, martini, port)	1
1 glass of table wine	1
1 pint of beer	2
1 can of beer	1½
1 bottle of 'super' or 'special' lager	2½
1 can of 'super' or 'special' lager	4
1 bottle of table wine	7
1 litre bottle of table wine	10
1 bottle of fortified wine (sherry, martini, port)	14
1 bottle of spirits (whisky, gin, vodka)	30

There are also many different kinds of beers, lagers and ciders sold in bottles and cans, and the tables on pages 25–6 show how many units they contain. It is important to remember that a pint of beer contains as much alcohol as a double whisky, a can of special lager contains the same as two double whiskies.

Alcohol in the bloodstream

GRAHAM:

After we got married Susan landed herself a good job running a local employment bureau. A car

HOW MANY UNITS IN YOUR DRINK?

Beers and lagers

Ordinary strength beer or lager	½ pint	1
	1 pint	2
	1 can	1½
Export beer	1 pint	2½
	1 can	2
Strong ale or lager	½ pint	2
	1 pint	4
	1 can	3
Extra strength beer or lager	½ pint	2½
	1 pint	5
	1 can	4

Ciders

Average Cider	½ pint	1½
	1 pint	3
	quart	
	bottle	6
Strong cider	½ pint	2
	1 pint	4
	quart	
	bottle	8

came with the job. But everyone working there goes for a drink after work, so she joined in. I've challenged her about drinking and driving, but she says she makes sure she's under the limit. Last night she had a night out with the girls and got a lift home but went straight to bed, obviously very drunk. This morning she seemed shaky but she still drove the car to the supermarket.

The amount of alcohol in the bloodstream is called the Blood Alcohol Concentration (usually shortened to BAC). This is measured as the number of milligrammes of alcohol in every 100 millilitres of blood (written as mg per cent). The legal driving limit in Britain is 80 mg per cent (about five single whiskies). As you will know, alcohol can also be measured in the breath. The equivalent legal limit on the breathalyser is 35 microgrammes (mcg) per cent. People's driving ability is affected soon after the first drink.

BAC	HOW YOU FEEL	HOW YOU BEHAVE
40	Begin to feel relaxed.	Increased chance of accidents.
60	Cheerful.	Poor judgment. Decisions may be affected.
80	Feelings of warmth and well being.	Some loss of inhibitions and self control. Slow reaction time. Driving definitely worse.
120	Talkative, excited and emotional.	Uninhibited, may act on impulse.
150	Silly and confused.	Speech slurred. May be aggressive.
200	Just plain drunk.	Staggering, double vision, loss of memory.
300		Unconsciousness possible.
400		Unconsciousness likely. Death not unknown.
500		Death possible.
600		Death probable.

The table on page 27 shows the changes we can expect at different BAC levels. But because of 'tolerance' to alcohol your partner may not seem to get drunk so easily.

The chances of having an accident are doubled at a BAC of only 40 (2 units). Someone who'd been involved in a heavy evening drinking session, amounting to, say, drinking three quarters of a bottle of whisky, would be well over the British limit *the following morning* as they drive to work.

So refusing to be a passenger in a car when the driver has been drinking is a good rule to stick to, as is the slogan DON'T DRINK & DRIVE.

WHAT IS SAFE DRINKING?

There is no level or kind of drinking that is completely safe for everyone. Remember that we all respond differently to alcohol. The limits below have been given by the Royal College of Psychiatrists. They are upper limits and it is not in any way being suggested that people drink up to this amount in any one week. Nor is it suggested that these amounts be concentrated into one or two drinking 'sessions'.

For Men	*For Women*	*For Pregnant Women*
Up to 21 Units per week	Up to 14 Units per week	Up to 6 Units per week (although in the United States and in Sweden, pregnant women are advised to drink no alcohol at all)

Safe drinking is not just about how *much* people drink.
It is about *how* they drink. It is about eating before or
during drinking and about not just *relying* on alcohol
for enjoyment.

It is helpful not to get caught up in buying rounds
in a bar or pub. Often you will end up having six drinks
– where two would have been fine – only because you
are with five other people. Give your body a complete
rest from alcohol on two or three days each week.

Making every other drink a non-alcoholic one is a
good way of slowing down your drinking.

Alcohol feeds into feelings of anxiety and depression
and makes things feel much worse so it's best to drink
when you're feeling good and on top of things.

Drinking is more risky for women because they have
more fat and less water in their bodies. Measure for
measure, they get drunker faster and feel the effects for
longer. During ovulation and menstruation the alcohol
stays in the bloodstream longer, so because of the
physical health risks involved, safe limits for women
are much lower than for men (see page 28).

Pregnant women in particular are advised to keep
their drinking down to two units, two or three times a
week. Better still, stop drinking completely if you're
pregnant and don't go above the limits for pregnancy
if you go on to breastfeed your baby.

Finally, there are times when you should avoid
drinking altogether: at work, when driving, when using
machinery and when looking after babies or small
children.

YOUR OWN DRINKING

Perhaps you don't drink at all, or at least never with your partner. It may be that your partner's drinking has put you off alcohol entirely, or perhaps you enjoy an occasional drink on your own or with friends as a treat.

Alternatively, you might have found that your drinking has increased. While your partner may still drink a lot more, you may be starting to experience some problems yourself.

Many women who seek help with a drinking problem have partners who are excessive drinkers.

Jennifer got on well with Jim until he started drinking excessively in the evenings. Then he really began to change. He seemed to be trying to annoy her, accusing her of looking a mess, flirting with her brother-in-law and not being strict enough with the children.

> For a while I tried to reason with Jim, but he just ignored me. Then I found that once I'd had my usual two or three drinks with him on a Saturday night, I could stand up to him. It got rid of a lot of the bad feelings I'd been bottling up, but last weekend I went a bit over the top and he slapped me across the face in front of our daughter. Things feel worse now, and I'm tempted to have a few drinks on my own when Jim's down at the club. I probably had too much last night because I didn't wake up in time to take my little girl to nursery school. But then my drinking's nothing compared with the amount Jim knocks back most nights.

SUMMARY

Knowing more about alcohol and the way it affects people should help you understand some of the ways in which it is affecting your partner. You should also be able to work out how much your partner is drinking. You should look at your own drinking too, and decide how to prevent it causing you problems in the future.

The next chapter considers the problems drinking can cause, and how these could be affecting your partner. But first try the following quiz on alcohol and test your newfound expertise.

WHAT DO YOU KNOW ABOUT ALCOHOL?

1.   Women get drunk more easily than men.

                     True   False

2.   Which of the following things will affect how quickly you get drunk?

                     Your weight

                     When you last ate

                     Mixing your drinks

3.   Alcohol spreads through the body very slowly.

                     True   False

4.   How many units are there in two glasses of sherry?

One   Two   Three

5. A single whisky contains more alcohol than
    a glass of wine.

    True   False

6. Alcohol contains:

    Proteins

    Carbohydrates

    Vitamins

7. How long does it take the body to get rid of
    the alcohol in two pints of beer?

    One hour

    Two hours

    Four hours

8. Which Blood Alcohol Concentration (BAC)
    is the legal driving limit in Britain?

    50

    80

    120

9. At which BAC is it possible to die?

    300

    400

    500

How much did you know?

1. True

2. All of them

3. False

4. Two

5. False

6. Carbohydrates

7. Four hours

8. 80

9. 500

3

YOUR PARTNER AND ALCOHOL

The more that you know about alcohol, the more accurately you can judge how much your partner is drinking, and how he or she is being affected by it. By the end of this chapter you should be clearer about how far his or her problems are caused by the drinking, and you will have a better picture of how you have been affected.

WHAT KINDS OF PEOPLE DRINK TOO MUCH?

It is often thought that people who drink too much are different from everyone else. This makes it harder for us to accept that someone we know well, respect, and care for, has allowed alcohol to get the better of him. Sometimes, insufficient knowledge about the effects of alcohol can prevent our recognising the problem – even in someone with whom we live or work. But *anyone* who drinks alcohol has a potential problem.

Joyce kept telling herself that Brian's problems couldn't be caused by drinking alone.

> Brian's not the type to let drink get the better of him. He's a sensible, strong-minded person who can usually cope with anything. Right now he's going through a run of bad luck. Once he's back on his feet again, he's bound to cut his drinking down.

Facts about *PROBLEM DRINKERS*

- Most are still at work and with their families.
- Many don't drink every day.
- Morning drinking is unusual.
- Now that alcohol is cheap and easy to buy it has become easier for people to drink too much. One need not be overwhelmed by special problems or worries to become a problem drinker.
- It doesn't take long to develop a problem. Younger people are as much at risk as older long-term drinkers.
- The fact that someone never gets drunk does not mean their drinking is under control.
- Problem drinkers are not 'ill' – although drinking can cause health problems.
- Many people can change their drinking habits without the benefit of outside help.
- Many problem drinkers change by stopping altogether, but others are equally successful at limiting their drinking.

If you've ever questioned the amount your partner drinks, you may have received this sort of reply: 'Yes I know I like a drink, but there's no way you can call me an alcoholic'. If your partner thinks of an alcoholic as someone who sleeps rough on park benches or under railway arches, then he or she has a point. But 95% of problem drinkers are not like this, nor are many of them *addicts* as such.

There are people whose problems come mainly from getting drunk and then into trouble with their families or with the police. Yet at other times, these same people may stay completely clear of alcohol for days or weeks.

There are others who drink frequently and in quantity, though perhaps not throughout the day. They may become tired and irritable, and certainly they run the risk of health problems and other complications.

Finally, some people drink all the time because their bodies have become so accustomed to alcohol that stopping or cutting down makes them feel ill. These drinkers will be shaky in the morning and may take an early morning drink to help them face the day. Your partner may think problem drinkers are all addicted in this way, but this is not the case: only a minority are unable to cope without alcohol and suffer from withdrawal symptoms when they stop drinking.

There are many different types of problem which can be caused by excessive drinking, and these are just a few of the more common examples that can occur.

HARRY:

I have tried to be a good husband to Ann. I'm fairly quiet, I try to please people, and I work hard at my job. For the past three years Ann's had problems with her nerves, and I don't know how to help. She's never the same from one day to the next, and has lost quite a bit of weight. She's never as nicely turned out, and goes out drinking twice a week with the women from the office.

Yesterday my team from the building site were all 'called off' through bad weather. I got home very early to find Ann asleep on the settee. I thought she'd been drinking, but wasn't certain. When she woke up she looked dreadful, and seemed embarrassed to see me. But I wasn't sure she'd been drinking, and I just can't pluck up the courage to say anything to her about how worried I feel.

HOW MUCH DOES YOUR PARTNER DRINK?

Think of a week when you have spent a lot of time with your partner. This means you're well placed to know roughly how much alcohol was consumed. Choose a week not too long ago – last week if possible. But don't choose a week when for some reason, like Christmas, your partner was drinking a good deal more or less than usual.

Next, think about each day of that week, and count the *units* of alcohol that your partner drank. You may have to add some units that you didn't see being consumed, but which you suspect were drunk, in view of what you've learned about your partner's pattern of drinking. If you're in doubt, don't add anything. Write down the units for each day, using the table on page 25 as a guide. Then add them up to give you the week's total.

Finally, check your total with the totals below. These totals are *dangerous levels of drinking.*

Anyone drinking above these levels is likely to be having problems and is taking serious risks with his or her health. Many people drinking *below* these levels may also have problems.

FOR MEN   FOR WOMEN

56 Units per week   35 Units per week

HOW DOES YOUR PARTNER USE ALCOHOL?

People with drinking problems use alcohol in different ways. Ask yourself the following questions:

- Does your partner try and keep the amount he or she drinks a secret?
- Has your partner ever hidden drink?
- Does your partner want to keep drinking when others stop?
- Does he or she get upset when people comment on his or her drinking?
- Does he or she usually drink more than he or she says they're going to?
- Does he or she forget things which happened while drinking?
- Does he or she drink faster than other people you know?
- Is your partner reluctant to go out or to meet people if he or she won't be able to drink at the time?

- Does your partner help him or herself to drinks, or buy drinks between rounds?
- Is your partner drinking more now than last year?
- Has your partner promised to stop or cut down and failed?
- Do the people your partner drinks with now drink more than the people he or she drank with before?
- Does your partner drink a lot without appearing to get drunk?

If you have answered YES to any one of these questions, you can be sure that your partner's drinking is a cause for concern.

KAREN:

I've noticed that Roddy's far less interested these days in doing anything or going anywhere unless there's going to be an opportunity to drink. He took me and the baby to the seaside yesterday but he was off to the local pub for a lunchtime drink once he'd got us settled. In the pub the other night I watched him closely, and I'm sure he ordered himself a double every time it was his round. He's also inclined to have one or two drinks at home *before* we go to the pub. He never did that a year ago.

PROBLEMS THAT DRINKING CAN CAUSE

Drinking too much can cause many kinds of problems and changes in your partner's life. The worksheet on pages 40–1 lists all the things known to be caused by harmful drinking. By checking through it you may find that behaviour which you found difficult to understand in the past has been caused by drinking. But long *before* many of these patterns occur, a person's drinking may become a serious problem.

TICK THE THINGS WHICH APPLY

Many of these problems will have upset you, and you may have been blamed for some of them. The following chapter suggests ways in which to cope with this situation so that *you* begin to feel stronger, and start to help yourself *and* your partner.

Health Problems

Tiredness
Depression
Irritability and moodiness
Night sweating
Sleeping problems
Weight gain or loss
Bruising and burns
Ulcers
Liver damage
Stomach upsets
Diarrhoea

Problems at Home

Money worries
Bad atmosphere
Problems with the police
Falling out with friends and neighbours
Selfishness
Arguments
Loss of interest in home life

Problems at Work

Arguments, falling out with the boss
Lateness
Job hopping
Accidents
Disciplinary action
Work absences
Dislike of workmates

Behaviour problems

Forgetfulness
Abuse
Seeking out drinking friends
Interest loss: in hobbies, sports etc.
Mood and behaviour changes

Problems in Relationships

Jealousy
Belief that partner is unfaithful
Feeling others are 'against you'
Loss of interest in sex
Impotence in men
Constant criticism of partner
Suspicion and lack of trust in others
Broken promises

DOES YOUR PARTNER NEED HELP?

By now, you will have formed a picture of the problems and changes in your partner's life, of his or her drinking pattern, and how it affects your relationship.

If you are still not sure about the extent to which these problems are caused by alcohol ask yourself these questions:

1.   *Are you convinced by your partner's assertion that he or she drinks only because of specific problems?*

This may be a genuine reaction, but drinking to cope with problems like depression and anxiety can only make the situation worse. Drinking may begin as an attempt to cope with loneliness, boredom, worries, shyness or just feeling upset. Other people can press us to drink more, more frequently, but a dangerous level of drinking should be tackled as a problem in its own right, no matter how the drinker tries to justify it.

2.   *Are you refusing to admit there is a real problem because you don't know what to do?*

This book should help you to decide what you can do or say, and cut out any nagging doubts. You can contact the organisations on pages 155–61 for further help.

3.   *Would it help to talk to someone?*

A trusted friend, or a member of your family, might be able to give you the support you need. If you do not want to tell anyone you know, you might consider talking to an alcohol counsellor. There are helpful addresses listed on pages 155–6.

GRAHAM:

I got so worried about Susan's drinking and driving, I couldn't sleep. I could see she wasn't the same person she used to be, but I didn't know what to put down to drinking. The main problem was she just refused to talk about it. I felt I couldn't trust my own judgement any more, and had to get some kind of professional advice. I found a number to ring in the telephone directory and have arranged to talk everything over with a counsellor tomorrow. I'm still worried but I feel I've done something positive.

SUMMARY

Anyone who drinks can develop a problem. If you've realised that your partner has a problem, you probably now see that his or her behaviour does make sense. But if you're still uncertain about this, do consider talking to someone close to you or to a professionally trained helper. You will find useful addresses on pages 155–61.

4
COPING
WITH
DRINKING

By now you should know more about alcohol and the problems it can cause. Hopefully you have been able to make more sense of your own feelings about trying to cope with your partner's drinking and subsequent behaviour. This is the time to turn to the reasons why you may have picked up this book in the first place – that is, to find out how to encourage your partner to change.

Although no-one can guarantee change, there are some things you can do to alter the way that *you* cope with the drinking and so make change more likely. These things will probably help you feel better, too. By the end of this chapter you may well have decided how you want to change your behaviour towards the drinker.

Your ability to carry out these decisions will be strengthened once you've completed the exercises in Chapter 5 which are designed to help you get more out of life, whatever your partner decides to do.

TRYING TO SURVIVE THE EFFECTS

People try to cope with someone else's drinking in many different ways, but mostly 'coping' means that their relationships with other people, particularly with their family, begin to change. People may be secretly worried and frightened, yet never speak about the problem, particularly in the early stages, when every attempt is made to believe that the cause of the problem is anything *but* drinking.

The stigma and shame that surround drinking problems and 'alcoholism' also stop people from revealing their worries, even to those whom they trust. Partners of problem drinkers often make elaborate attempts to put on a brave face for the benefit of the outside world. Sooner or later, when it becomes impossible to keep up the charade, the partner decides to avoid social life altogether and to break off contact with their friends and family.

MARGARET:

I've tried to take a lot of pride in myself as a wife and mother. I'm worried about what people would think if they found out about Sam's drinking and the problems it's causing. So I don't encourage people to visit us any more, and I end up phoning Sam's office with an excuse if he can't get into work. I like to stay in more in the evenings because Sam drinks less when I'm around. As for going out with him – well that's 'not on' any more because the last time he just made a laughing stock of himself.

Often, the drinker can no longer be trusted with

responsibility. Forgetfulness becomes commonplace, and promises are broken regularly. Children can feel let down, and may be embarrassed by, and ashamed of, the drinker's behaviour.

Children may spend less time at home, or retreat into their own shells. It is common for children and the non-drinking partner to take over responsibility for the things the drinker is neglecting. A partner may end up getting a job or working longer hours in order to bring in more money whilst the oldest child may watch over the younger children. Sometimes the family gets on with life as if the drinker didn't exist. The questionnaire on pages 49–65 will help you see exactly how *you* have been trying to cope with the drinking problem.

WHY DRINKERS OFTEN DENY THE PROBLEM

Many drinkers genuinely believe that they don't need to change. They cannot accept any link between drinking and their problems, and see nothing unusual in their pattern of drinking. Other drinkers, however, know deep down that they have a problem, but work very hard at ignoring the need to change their habits. Understanding that our behaviour causes problems is not always followed by a desire to change it. There can be many reasons for this. For example:

- Fear of 'owning up' to problems and being ridiculed by other people.
- Wanting to avoid the guilt which goes with accepting responsibility.
- Believing that we can't change.
- Fear of what change could mean.
- Fear of failure.

- Fear of being rejected by loved ones.
- Believing that nothing good will come out of it.

If you share some of these beliefs with the drinker, you often end up playing down the problems or hoping they will sort themselves out without your needing to do anything. Maybe you point to other people who seem to be in more trouble but who are allowed to get away with it. You may work hard at building up an image of yourself or your relationship, saying 'We're OK – but other people misjudge us'.

If you want the drinker to change, you have to help convince him or her that change is really necessary. You also have to help him to accept that it will be worthwhile. The drinker needs to feel confident that he *can* change, and to believe that it will not be too painful.

Trying to support the drinker in these ways can be very hard, especially when *you* are the one being hurt. You may feel that you lack the strength particularly if your affections for, and trust in, the drinker have been badly damaged.

JOHN:

I began to realise that going on at my son Robert about not trying hard enough to get a job and showing how much I disapproved of his friends and his appearance, was driving him away from me. I'm now trying to talk to him more, through the week when he's not drinking, without putting him down like I used to. It's hard but he'll probably never listen to what I have to say about his drinking unless we can build up some respect for each other.

HOW DO YOU COPE?

Just as we are changed by other people's behaviour, so the drinker is changed by ours. Even 'ignoring' the drinking will have its effects.

Some of your reactions may be an attempt to protect yourself and others. There may be other things you do which try to influence the drinking directly. You may react at certain times or when particular things are happening. You may have special reasons for what you do.

The following questionnaire will help you to judge your reactions to drinking and to make decisions about how to react in the future. The questionnaire is divided up into four worksheets entitled 'How Do I React to Drinking?', 'What Do I React Against?', 'When Do I React?', and 'Why Do I React The Way I Do?'.

Circle 'seldom' or 'often' after each question, whichever best applies to your situation. Opposite each worksheet there are some established views about 'Reacting to Drinking'. The question numbers appear before each heading. Circle those to which you have answered 'often', and then make notes at the bottom of the worksheet concerning the reactions you think you ought to modify.

HOW DO YOU REACT?

1.	I threaten to leave.	Seldom	Often
2.	I plead with him/her.	Seldom	Often
3.	I take no notice.	Seldom	Often
4.	I go away for a while.	Seldom	Often
5.	I get on with my own life.	Seldom	Often
6.	I make excuses for him/her to other people.	Seldom	Often
7.	I protect him/her from harming him/herself.	Seldom	Often
8.	I tell him/her to get help.	Seldom	Often
9.	I talk to someone else about it.	Seldom	Often
10.	I join him/her in drinking.	Seldom	Often
11.	I hide drink or pour it away.	Seldom	Often
12.	I discuss with him/her the reasons for drinking too much.	Seldom	Often

Now check your answers with the information over the page marking the numbers where you have given the answer 'often'. When you have done this record your decisions below about how to react differently in the future.

Things I Feel I Should Do **MORE** Often

Things I Feel I Should Do **LESS** Often

HOW *SHOULD* YOU REACT?

OK

(9) Involving Others

Explaining to people you trust that there is a drinking problem can help you cope with anxiety. They probably suspect anyway and there are many ways they could help.

(5) Getting On With Living

Keeping up interests, activities and friendships that matter to you and bring enjoyment, will keep you strong in spite of the drinking.

(8) Challenging

Challenging your partner about the problems caused by the drinking means that the situation can't be ignored. The more often you do this the less rewarding drinking becomes. But simply getting angry may not solve anything (see pages 15–17, Chapter 1). You should be showing it is the problem drinking that makes you feel angry, but that you still care about your partner. He/she needs to know that you're not prepared to keep putting up

Questionable

(1) Threatening

Empty threats encourage the drinker to take no notice of what you say. Carrying out a threat to leave until he gets help can be useful – but it takes guts and careful planning. For help with this see page 119.

(2) Pleading

It's important that you let your partner know how strongly you feel about the problem. But, he/she needs to know you mean it.

(11) Removing Drink

This might help because it shows how strongly you feel. On the other hand, it suggests that you don't expect him/her to be responsible for the drinking.

(7) Protecting

This is a natural reaction. But, it stops the drinker from seeing the true consequences of the drinking. Protection from discomfort

Avoid It!

(10) Joining In

Joining in on the drinking may be your way of saying 'See if I care!' or 'This is how it feels to be on the receiving end!'. But it allows the drinker to point the finger at *you* when you're trying to challenge *his/her* drinking. Page 30 in Chapter 2 has some notes about your own drinking.

(3) Ignoring

Ignoring the drinking suggests to the drinker that you don't find it a problem. Sitting on the fence like this may feel comfortable, but it means a breakdown in communication. This may lead the drinker to feel that you don't care about it at all.

(6) Covering Up

'Covering up' (for example to the boss) means you're letting him/her get away with the consequences of his/her drinking. This can only encourage more drinking.

...take over the drinker's responsibilities.

(4) Withdrawing
Going away for a while could give you a breathing space to think. It could also mean a well-earned break. But, withdrawing from regular contact could look like you're *ignoring the problem.*

...talking about the reasons for drinking, and being sympathetic can encourage him/her to find excuses for difficult behaviour. This takes attention away from the need for change.

NOW GO BACK TO PAGE 49

WHAT DO YOU REACT AGAINST?

1. Any drinking at all.   Seldom   Often
2. Drinking when he or she has promised not
   to.   Seldom   Often
3. Only drinking which causes problems.   Seldom   Often
4. Situations which could lead to drinking.   Seldom   Often
5. Attitudes and things about him or her which
   cause drinking.   Seldom   Often
6. People and friends who encourage drinking. Seldom   Often

Now check your answers again with the information on pages 54–5, marking the numbers where you have given the answer 'often'. Then record your decisions below about how to react differently in the future.

WHAT Should I React Against **MORE?**

WHAT Should I React Against **LESS?**

WHAT *SHOULD* YOU REACT AGAINST?

OK	Questionable	Avoid It!

OK

(2) Broken Promises

Challenging your partner on this is positive action to be encouraged. You are not implying that you no longer care for him/her, or that you reject drinking altogether. What you *are* saying is that drinking too much provokes behaviour that you refuse to tolerate because it is harmful to everyone. You are saying that when he/she drinks more than X, Y invariably occurs and you are not prepared to put up with that!

(3) Harmful Drinking

Reacting only to drinking which leads to problems avoids the difficulties listed under 'Any Drinking'. It also makes excessive drinking less rewarding because he/she is being taken to task for it. On the other hand, 'safe and appropriate' drinking is tolerated

Questionable

(4) Drinking Situations

You will know what kinds of situations trigger problem drinking. It could be boredom, an argument, pay-day, a disappointment, or simply pressure from others to drink. Helping your partner to find different ways of coping without having to drink could help. But this isn't easy, and implying he/she is about to go on a drinking spree could anger your partner.

(6) Drinking Friends

It's very likely that the behaviour of your partner's drinking friends has a lot to do with his/her problem drinking. He/she may have a group of friends, at work or in the neighbourhood, who drink heavily on a regular basis and who press him/her to join them. You could approach them directly and try to discourage them, or you could

Avoid It!

(1) Any Drinking

Reacting against any drinking invites being seen as anti-drink and a kill-joy. (Of course your problems may have led you to become anti-drink.) More importantly, it implies that your partner can never have any control over alcohol.

(5) Attitudes

It's tempting to attack the character of someone who's causing us hurt and making us angry. It reflects the way we feel about them at that very moment (e.g. we think of them as thoughtless, unkind, selfish, spineless etc.) Reacting like this usually has the opposite effect of helping someone to change – he/she wants to dig his/her heels in all the more. So limit your criticisms to harmful drinking and behaviour, and broken promises, only when they lead to problem drinking.

simply point out to your partner that their drinking is excessive. You might also point out that he/she drinks more with them. However, your partner may resent your 'interference' in his/her social life.

and thus a better option. The point being made is that you have to be consistent.

NOW GO BACK TO PAGE 52

WHEN DO YOU REACT?

1.	When he/she is drinking.	Seldom	Often
2.	When I'm drinking.	Seldom	Often
3.	When I can't stand it any longer.	Seldom	Often
4.	When he/she starts an argument.	Seldom	Often
5.	When he/she has sobered up.	Seldom	Often
6.	When I can think straight about things.	Seldom	Often
7.	When I've been made really angry.	Seldom	Often
8.	When he/she is feeling remorseful.	Seldom	Often
9.	In front of other people.	Seldom	Often

Now check your answers again with the information over the page. Then record your decisions below about how to react differently in the future.

Good Times For Reacting

Bad Times For Reacting

WHEN *SHOULD* YOU REACT?

OK	Questionable	Avoid It!

OK

(5, 8) After A Serious Drinking Session

Your partner is more likely to take note of your challenges when sober and perhaps also remorseful following a serious drinking session. Opening up a discussion the following morning, before he/she has had the chance to work out ways of excusing and justifying the behaviour, is a good time to pick.

Questionable

(1, 2) While Drinking

Drinkers make many promises while drinking which are broken or forgotten once they have sobered up. Anyone's judgement is distorted by a few drinks, so this would not be a good time for you to try and reach an understanding with your partner either. But if he/she opens up a discussion, don't discourage it. Instead try and agree a time the next day to resume it.

Avoid It!

(3, 4, 7) When I'm Upset

When you are arguing with your partner about problems caused by drinking or when the problems caused by drinking are upsetting you, it is tempting to bring up the drinking problem. But you are more likely to say things about your partner that you will later regret so try to cool off before discussing drinking. – See section on 'Anger, Frustration and Resentment' in Chapter 1 (pages 15–17).

(1) During A Serious Drinking Session

Trying to tackle your partner when he/she's worse the wear for drink is dangerous and won't work. It could provoke a fight, and any promises will be totally forgotten by the next day.

(9) In Front Of Other People

You may want to bring up drinking in front of other people in the hope that they will give you moral support. Perhaps you feel also that your partner is more likely to discuss things rationally and coolly in the presence of others. To ask people whom your partner respects to challenge his drinking could prove helpful; however, to challenge him or her in front of them might make him/her feel cornered and betrayed.

(6) When I'm In Control

The best time for you to react is when your emotions are in check. Then you can resist any attempt to provoke your anger, your tears and so on. Explain that although you care for him/her, you find his/her behaviour intolerable. Be firm and frank. Since this is not easy to do don't worry if you don't get it right the first time!

NOW GO BACK TO PAGE 56

WHY DO YOU REACT THE WAY YOU DO?

1.	Because it gets rid of pent-up feelings.	Seldom	Often
2.	Because I want to shame him/her into taking some action.	Seldom	Often
3.	Because I want to get back at him/her.	Seldom	Often
4.	To show him/her what the drinking is like.	Seldom	Often
5.	To protect everyone from the consequences of the drinking.	Seldom	Often
6.	To encourage him/her to be a better person.	Seldom	Often
7.	To encourage him/her to drink much less.	Seldom	Often

Now check your answers again with the information over the page, marking those numbers to which you have answered 'often'. Record the decisions you have come to concerning how to behave differently in the future below.

Good Reasons For My Reactions

NOT such Good Reasons For My Reactions

GOOD REASONS FOR REACTING

OK

(7) To Change The Drinking

Aiming to change the pattern of your partner's drinking, so that it falls within safe limits (see Chapter 2) is a good goal to set. No one can dispute the requirement that people drink in a way harmless to themselves and others. There may be many difficulties in your relationship with your partner, but to change a destructive drinking pattern has to be the first priority.

(4) To Show Him/Her What The Drinking Is Like

Trying to help your partner to become aware of his/her drinking

Questionable

(1) To Feel Better

'Lashing out' and having a 'show down' in general may happen from time to time. It means that feelings are pent up on both sides. Usually, as a result, though, people feel worse about themselves after a quarrel and there are better ways of coping with negative feelings. See Chapters 1 and 5.

(5) To Protect Everyone

The result of excessive drinking is to put many people at risk. It can cause financial hardship, emotional distress, and real danger. If you are a parent naturally you will want to

Avoid It!

(6) To Change Him/Her

Few of us react well to demands that we change *the way we are*, although we may consider changing *some of the things we do* if the request is made by someone whom we know cares for us and is acting in our interests. Try to understand the hardships of having to change an established pattern and try also not to put your partner down too readily.

(3) To Get Back

A thirst for 'revenge' grips all of us from time to time. It is usually a response to a deep wound or pattern, and its consequences, is an important thing to aim for. Drinkers constantly try to play down the extent and costs of their drinking. Use the information in Chapter 2 to challenge your partner's views about his/her drinking. Explain that you have been given your information by an Alcohol Information & Advice Centre.

protect your children from harm, and often this consideration has to outweigh any desire to change the drinking pattern of a partner. This should not mean protecting your partner from the consequences. Nor should it mean your taking responsibility for everything.

betrayal. Never act hastily or cruelly. Your partner is likely to retaliate and try to hurt you even more deeply.

(2) To Shame Him/Her
Trying to shame someone into changing his/her behaviour rarely seems to work – it simply makes people feel worse about themselves.

NOW GO BACK TO PAGE 60

TAKING ACTION ON DRINKING: A PERSONAL CONTRACT

A personal contract is a promise we make with ourselves to carry something through to completion. You have made a number of decisions already about how to cope with drinking in future situations. If you summarise these decisions here, you can keep returning to this page to help you assess the progress you are making. But remember, change is no guarantee of success, and the most important changes to work on are discussed in the next chapter.

Things I intend to try to do: (check with page 49)

Things I shall try to take action on: (check with pages 52–3)

My reasons for acting on drinking are: (check with
pages 60–61)

The best times for taking action will be: (check with
pages 56–7)

IF YOUR PARTNER DECIDES TO DO SOMETHING ABOUT DRINKING

Your partner could respond to your pressure in any number of ways. For example by:

- saying he/she might do something
- saying he/she should do something
- promising to stop or cut down
- promising to get help sometime
- agreeing to talk to you about it
- agreeing to something, but only *if* you do something in return or *when* something has happened (e.g. 'when I've got through this bad time at work')

He or she may have said any or all of these things while drinking and you may have become very sceptical about your partner's sincerity. Even so, ask yourself: 'When he or she starts talking about the need for taking action on his or her drinking problem, what should *I* say and do?'

JENNIFER:

I realised that having a row with Jim when we'd both been drinking wasn't getting me anywhere. I knew I was drinking too much, and surprised myself by managing to give up completely for the time being, after which I felt much more in control of things. I learned not to ignore any problems being caused by Jim's drinking, always bringing them up the following morning. Eventually he broke down after a really bad night, and said he was fed up with it all as well. He promised to stop drinking and I was so relieved I left it at that. But now he's drinking again, and just says he'll do something about it after the summer holidays – that's three months away.

Don't beat about the bush

As soon as your partner starts talking about doing something about drinking, no matter how vaguely, it is important to be direct yet low key. The only time this doesn't apply strictly is during a drinking session. *If this is the case, be positive about the suggestions and fix a time for discussion, preferably for the first opportunity your partner is sober.*

What should you aim for?

Talking about doing something is never enough. You should aim to persuade your partner to take a specific course of action, to agree on *what* he or she ought to do, how to go about it and *when* to make a start. As soon as your partner is open to a discussion, and sober, argue firmly and positively for a decisive programme. He or she may change the subject, or may try to negotiate. Nevertheless keep repeating your message. For example:

Yes I know you're feeling upset about what happened at work yesterday, but since you've decided to do something about your drinking, let's work out where we can go for advice . . .

Sure you feel you'd like to cut down on your own,

and I believe you can do it, but there are good booklets we can write off for which advise on how best to cut down. Let's phone or write for them right now. (See page 163 for suggested booklets.)

I know you don't drink as much as many other people, but now that you've agreed to get help about your drinking, let's make an appointment with a counsellor.

By all means, volunteer to go with your partner to see a counsellor.

Should you compromise?

Your partner may agree to take a certain course of action only if you agree to do something in return. Try to work out whether such a compromise is advisable by answering the following questions:

- Is what is being asked of me reasonable and fair? Is it possible?
- Am I being asked to do this just to 'delay' things – or is this something that can help us both?
- Is there something I can offer to do in return which would ease things for my partner or for both of us?

If, for example, your partner wants a new job and promises to stop drinking as soon as he gets one, that is a non-starter. But if he wants you to stop criticising his appearance, and to stop telling him that he's useless, in return for promising to get help from a counsellor, *then* you have to ask serious questions about your lack of support for him. There may be things you can do and changes you can make, which will give your partner the incentive to stop or cut down drinking. But it is very important that you agree to make these changes *only after your partner has made the first move*.

Christine and her husband, Steve, ended up having a very frank discussion about their marriage after Steve opened up about his drinking. He agreed to stop drinking completely and to write away for some literature. He also agreed that he would go with Christine to see a counsellor if this didn't work.

> I knew within myself that there were some things in our marriage that were going wrong – but the drinking was getting in the way of discussing anything. So I've agreed to make some changes, which I'm prepared to work at as long as Steve's making an effort to change the drinking.

To stop drinking for a while, or to go for counselling for a few weeks, would count as a first move. At the back of the book are the addresses of organisations which supply information about local counselling services.

WHAT TO EXPECT

From hospitals and rehabilitation centres

Drinkers who are heavily dependent on alcohol may need help with 'withdrawals'. Many hospitals provide this but would expect the drinker to be committed to wanting to stop drinking. Some provide extra help through nurses, psychologists and social workers. This could involve counselling, group discussions, information sessions and help with practical problems. The length of stay will range from patient to patient. Sometimes, once the patient is physically fit, he or she will be asked to continue as a day patient.

There are also privately run residential centres, some of which expect the client to stay for several months. Here the emphasis is placed on helping the drinker to rebuild his or her life, and to learn how to stop drinking completely.

Once the drinker leaves a centre or hospital they have to begin to learn how to cope with the pressures of independent living. It is very important at this stage that they continue to receive professional help of some kind.

From Alcoholics Anonymous (AA)

Wherever you live you will be able to find a local AA group. The group is made up of ex-drinkers helping each other to cope with living without alcohol. Most newcomers will be expected to listen to a speaker talking about their drinking history, and how they have learned to stay sober. Afterwards there is time for discussion and for people to talk about their own experiences. Members are expected to follow twelve 'recovery steps' and to attend meetings regularly. Often they are encouraged to seek special help from a long-term member called a 'sponsor'.

Partners can attend AA's sister organisation, 'Al-Anon'. These groups are run in a similar way and are especially helpful to people who feel isolated. They offer reassurance and support, and a chance to talk about any problems.

From counselling

If you telephone and ask to see a counsellor, you will be given an appointment, to suit you, probably within a few days.

Counsellors are paid workers or volunteers who have been specially chosen and trained to work with problem drinkers and their partners. They will give you as much of their time as you need, or want, to discuss how to deal with your problems.

Drinkers and their partners should receive counselling from the *same* case worker in order to build up trusting, confidential, comfortable relationships. It is unlikely that you will be pressured to join a group.

The problem drinker will decide, with the counsellor's help, what to do about his/her drinking pattern. It may be enough to cut the drinking down, provided certain important rules are followed. Usually, though, the agreed aim is to stop drinking, at least for a while. One does not have to get medical help in order to stop drinking but this is sometimes the best procedure. Counsellors can advise you about this, and will usually be happy to help with other problems as well.

Many partners go along to counselling with the drinker – but the choice is up to each individual. To go along only to 'make sure your partner arrives on the doorstep' would not be very helpful. But by going along you can work out ways to help and support your partner, and to help yourself to cope with whatever difficulties arise.

HOPES AND DISAPPOINTMENTS

Neither your world nor your partner's will necessarily change because he or she has agreed to tackle the drinking problem. Sadly, not everyone can resolve a drinking problem, and some of those who do may slip from time to time, so be optimistic, but try also to be realistic.

If the drinking can be brought under control, the relationship should pick up again, but adjustments will have to be made also, which require thought and effort on your part, to make this period of your lives easier for both of you. Probably, for example, the drinker will become interested in matters which have not concerned him/her for some time, such as your method of paying bills, and if you have taken responsibility for these practical matters over a long period of time, it may not be easy for you to share decisions with your partner once again. This is the sort of conflict with which counsellors can help.

This chapter has shown how you can help your partner, but do remember – even if your partner can't change, things *can* get better for you. You are entitled to look for your own happiness.

KAREN:

When Roddy eventually went to see someone about his drinking, I was over the moon. I went with him to see the counsellor after that, and although I learned about how to help Roddy, I was told to prepare myself for any set-backs or 'relapses'. He stopped drinking completely for three months. but then started again at my sister's wedding.

Of course I was bitterly disappointed, but I knew it meant I had to go back to the contract I'd made with myself about coping with the drinking. I'm working on this again, and just trying to keep my own life going in spite of his drinking.

5

COPING
WITH LIFE

If you have worked through the book to this point, you have covered a good deal of ground and have learned about alcohol and its problems. You have made important decisions also about the way alcohol affects your partner and about how you react to his or her drinking. By now you have also taken steps to change the way you both deal with the bad feelings that drinking creates, as well as with the drinking problem itself, and hopefully you are beginning to feel more in control of your own life and more optimistic about changing things.

This chapter is about being good to yourself. Its aim is to help you discover what changes you must make in order to get more out of your own life, what your priorities are and what you want to do with your life. When you have learned how to sort out your own goals, you may want to pass some tips on to any children you may have, so that they in turn can learn to improve their lives, despite their parent's drinking problem. There are specific guidelines for children in Chapter 6.

Allow yourself plenty of time to work through the chapter. Don't try to tackle all the changes you plan to make straight away. Put the ideas you want to follow in one section into action before reading the next section. Slow down a bit if the pace seems too fast. Should things get difficult, turn to the advice in Chapter 7.

UNHELPFUL CHANGES

In the previous chapter you learned to pinpoint some of the negative things you do in reaction to your partner's drinking. Many of these things were damaging to you as well as unlikely to help your partner. For example:

Covering up

If you have been pretending to relatives, neighbours and friends that family problems are nothing to do with drinking you have been putting yourself under enormous strain. By cheating ourselves of the release that comes from speaking honestly and openly with the people we love, we unnecessarily increase the strain we are under.

Holding back from people

The partners of drinkers often avoid embarrassing, difficult situations by avoiding the people who matter to them. In turn, their children may be reluctant to bring friends home, in case the drinking parent causes trouble. This is unfortunate because it is vital to our well-being to have relationships with people we care for and respect. They are our best life-lines in difficult times and by letting these relationships go, we risk feeling even more helpless, hopeless, bewildered and depressed.

Losing interest in things around you

Harry used to be very active in his union until he started to worry about Ann's drinking.

> When I got back from a union meeting, Ann had always had a good drink. If I passed a comment, she'd just complain about me going out at night and leaving her on her own. I ended up dropping the meetings so I could keep an eye on her. In any case, I used to worry so much about what Ann was getting up to, I couldn't concentrate on the business of the meeting. But at the same time I felt very resentful about it – and now I'm pretty sure she's drinking through the day.

Sometimes so much time and effort is spent trying to protect everyone from the drinking problem, that there seems to be no time left over for doing the things you enjoy. Some of these things may have to be abandoned because there is less money to go round, but there may be small, inexpensive activities, like walking in the park or listening to music, which give just as much pleasure and if these activities are dropped you cheat yourself of all enjoyment.

Joining the drinking

Sometimes partners try to cope with their own stress by over-indulging in drinking as well, or by using other drugs, like tranquillisers, sleeping pills or tobacco, as a 'crutch'. In the long run this can undermine your sense of being in control of situations and cause serious personal problems. Ways to check whether you are in danger of abusing drugs are listed on page 162.

CATHIE:

I went to the doctor and told him all about Mum. He said he wished I'd come before, because it would have helped him to approach her health problems differently – he's Mum's doctor as well. He says that the next time she comes to see him, he's going to ask her about her drinking, but he won't mention I've been to see him about it. I'd really gone to see him about getting some pills for my nerves, but he wasn't happy about the idea at all. He only gave me enough for four days, but said I should see him again in a fortnight for a chat if I was still feeling bad. He agreed with my sister that I was far too involved in Mum's life, and not looking after myself enough.

BEING GOOD TO YOURSELF

This chapter deals with how to make life better for yourself. Various ways are listed below. Whether your problems are big or small, you can only gain by working through them.

1. Finding things to enjoy
2. Building good relationships
3. Dealing with depression
4. Coping with anxiety
5. Making decisions
6. Solving problems
7. Making plans for the future

Each of these items is discussed in a separate section. Remember to work on no more than one section at a time.

1. Finding things to enjoy

There are many reasons why it is important for you to spend time on yourself. For example:

- To keep from brooding on the drinking problem.
- To help you unwind and relax.
- To give you an opportunity to learn how to do new things, and to meet people.
- To be 'yourself' for a change – not just someone else's parent, partner or friend.
- To discover new things about yourself.
- To compensate for the stress created by the problems you are coping with.
- To reward yourself for dealing with the difficult events and monotonous aspects of your life.

Agnes found life generally unrewarding, between watching over a demanding toddler and worrying about her husband Gavin's drinking.

My little boy sleeps very little at night, and is

constantly on the go all day. I've no family in the area to help me, and Gavin isn't interested in helping much. There doesn't seem to be the time or energy for things that interest me. At some stage over the weekend we always have a showdown about the drinking. He says he'll cut down, but I can't pin him down as to how he's going to go about it.

But things feel a bit better now because I've started 'keep-fit' classes again after joining a baby-sitting circle. The classes are held at the community centre, and I've discovered a lot of other activities which are run there that I might be able to join as well. I'm glad I took some action, because looking back on it I think I was on the verge of serious depression.

The worksheets that follow on pages 80–6 are designed to help you list all the things you can think of which might bring you enjoyment, so work at your own pace, follow the instructions.

2. Building good relationships

As we have seen, while you have been trying to cope with your partner's drinking problems you may have lost touch with the people who matter to you. This may have happened so slowly that you haven't even realised how much your life has changed. Remember that friendships and relationships are vital to one's own balance and well-being.

(Continued on page 87.)

FINDING THINGS TO ENJOY: WORKSHEET

Fill in the following lists: *Don't worry to start with whether or not you can do the things you list.* Then tick the columns on the right side of the page, and go to complete the next worksheet.

WORKSHEET

Things I used to enjoy a long time ago but don't do now	When could you do them? (Tick ONE of the columns)		
	Now	*Sometime*	*Never*
1.			
2.			
3.			
4.			
5.			
6.			
7.			
8.			

**Things I've always wanted
to do but have never tried**

**When could you do them?
(Tick ONE of the columns)**

Now   *Sometime*   *Never*

1.

2.

3.

4.

5.

6.

7.

8.

'IT'S IMPOSSIBLE!'

Now, transfer all the items you have listed in the 'Never' column of the previous worksheet to this worksheet. In the right-hand column now enter '1' beside the most difficult activity, '2' beside the next most difficult activity, and so on down the line in descending order.

Things I think I can never do   **How difficult are they?**

1.

2.

3.

4.

5.

6.

7.

Now write the two least difficult things below (i.e. the two highest numbered items you have listed), along with the reasons why they seem difficult to you now.

The two least difficult things   **Why they are difficult**

1.

2.

(Later in this chapter you will learn ways to tackle the obstacles you've listed in the right-hand column.)

AN ACTIVITY LIST FOR THE MONTHS AHEAD

This sheet is your record of how you plan to widen your activities and horizons. Write down three things that you enjoy doing now, and to which you'd like to devote more time. Choose three things from the 'now' column on pages 81–2, and three more things from the 'sometime' column; add these to your list. When making your choices, try to bear in mind how much money and time are involved, as well as how keen you are to try these activities.

Things to do More of

1.

2.

3.

New Things to Start Now

1.

2.

3.

New Things to Start Later

1.

2.

3.

On the sheets that follow, write an outline of day-by-day steps to help you carry through your 'activity list'. Make sure you enter plans for 'later' things in these diary sheets too. Go back to these sheets, from time to time, to monitor your progress.

ACTIVITY DIARY SHEET

Record the steps of your plan to take up more enjoyable activities here on this worksheet. We have listed one or two examples to get you started. Write the month in, above, and the days of the month down on the left-hand column side.

Month: **Activity plan**

1st   day

2nd   day   e.g. Phone Margaret about a day out.

3rd   day

4th   day

5th   day   e.g. Find out what activities are on offer at the
                           Sports Club.

6th   day

7th   day   e.g. Get books from the library.

8th   day

9th   day

10th   day

11th   day

12th   day

13th   day

14th   day

15th   day

16th   day

17th   day

18th   day

19th   day

20th   day

21st   day

22nd   day

23rd   day

24th   day

25th   day

26th   day

27th   day

28th   day

29th   day

30th   day

31st   day

Now copy or redesign diary sheets for use next month, or use your own diary.

Why we lose touch with people

At different times in our lives our involvement with other people changes. As children, we don't choose our parents and can't always choose our other relationships. If we settle down with a partner, we may feel that the closeness, affection, trust and things we share in this primary relationship cancel our need to have other relationships. Sometimes we stop seeing other people because there is jealousy, and we want to reassure our partner. In abusive relationships, it is common for the abused partner to be completely isolated. This puts her even more at risk because she totally depends on this one relationship. If you are isolated in an abusive relationship please consider contacting Women's Aid or an Advice Bureau immediately. Organisations which specialise in helping abused women are also listed at the back of the book (see page 161).

Another reason for losing touch with our friends is that not much time and energy remain after we've dealt with all our work and domestic commitments. You may end up doing many of the chores which used to be your partner's responsibility. If this applies to you, remember that, while some things must be done, to take over all the responsibility may simply clear the way for your partner to drink even more.

JENNIFER:

Eventually I managed to pin Jim down after another bad bout of drinking – lasting all weekend and leaving him unfit for work on the Monday. He agreed to see a counsellor on the Wednesday, and I went along, too, and had a chat with the counsellor on my own. She helped me realise I'd been too soft on Jim. As well as holding down a job, I'd had sole responsibility for the children and was doing all the other things about the house Jim used to share with me.

She made me see that there was no way Jim would be able to be fully responsible for himself when I couldn't trust him with anything. In any case, I'd ended up with no spare time in my life to do the things I liked doing – like visiting my family and playing golf and tennis. I'm still worried about Jim having a lot to do with money though.

Finally, we lose touch in order to save ourselves from having to account for the problems caused by drinking. You may have felt it was too painful and personal to admit to people that your partner cannot control his or her drinking. Opting out from relationships so as to spare yourself explanations and embarrassing situations may seem easier, but this 'solution' is at your own expense. Since some friends will give up on you, you rob yourself of your key source of comfort and security: friendship.

CATHIE:

I felt badly let down by my sister Sonia. We were

always close, even after she married and went to live twenty-five miles away. But then we fell out over Mum. You could have predicted it really – she said I was doing far too much for her, and I accused her of being uncaring. Then she sided with my husband and they both got angry with me about neglecting the kids and spending too much time at Mum's. She said Mum was an alcoholic and would never stop drinking. She's upset me so much I just don't bother keeping in touch with her any more.

Why friendship matters

Friendship is very important, for some of the reasons listed below. Please read it, and then go on to add some thoughts of your own. While filling in this worksheet think back to the friendships you have had in the past, as well as to the good friends you have now.

- Planning and doing things with someone whose company you enjoy.
- Laughing, having fun, and forgetting problems for a while.
- Talking seriously with someone you trust and whose opinion you value.
- Looking back on shared good times.
- Experiencing a different lifestyle through someone else.
- Giving and receiving help, advice and support.
- Hearing a different viewpoint on things.
- Sharing day-to-day thoughts and experiences.
- Knowing someone cares for you despite your faults.

Now add your own thoughts about friendship:

John received a phone call, out of the blue, from an old university friend who suggested having a reunion at the university club with some other friends from their student days. John's first instinct was to not go, because worries about his son and other recent problems which had cropped up at work were getting him down but some other instinct made him decide to go.

Going down to the club after such a long time was like a breath of fresh air. It was amazing how I could pick up with people after three years. We all had a good laugh together about old times, and for at least two hours I hardly gave any thought to the things that had been bothering me. The only relaxation I normally have is potting plants in the greenhouse, or reading a good book. This was a far better tonic. There was someone I met at the Club for the first time who's a lecturer at the university. I've arranged to have a day out fishing with him.

Making new friends

Making new friends isn't easy. Even good, long-standing relationships run into difficulties, from time to time.

Some people avoid getting close to others because they are frightened of getting hurt. They are frightened of having their trust betrayed, of being taken advantage of, of being misunderstood or rejected. There is also the fear they may be deeply hurt should a close friendship end, so to protect themselves from ever being hurt, some people avoid close friendships altogether. They rob themselves of the benefits of friendship, which make it worth taking these risks.

Beginning new friendships, when you have been isolated for a long time, may not be easy, but answering the following questions may help you:

1. What qualities, in your opinion, are to be found in a 'good friend'?
2. Of the people you already know, which ones might be open to a closer relationship?
3. What steps would you take to build a real friendship out of a casual relationship?
4. How might you go about making contact with the family members and friends with whom you have lost touch since your partner's drinking got bad?
5. How can you start to meet new people?

Here are 6 tips that may help:

- Help people to feel that you find them interesting and worthy of your respect.
- Don't try to be someone that you're not. Just be yourself.
- Show that you can see other people's points of view.
- Be honest and forthcoming (but not totally open with everyone).
- Don't be critical, 'pushy' or possessive.
- Make the other person feel at ease.

Julie's husband lost his job in a bakery three years ago. Since then his drinking has increased a lot. They're both in their late forties, with a grown-up family.

I don't seem to be able to get through to Sydney about his drinking, even though it's obvious his health is affected. Now the supermarket I've worked in for two years has been taken over, and I've lost my job too. We've got other problems – trying to get the housing authority to do something about the damp in the house, and my daughter who's schizophrenic and in hospital just now.

The good thing is I've made a new friend out of someone I met at the health centre a few weeks ago. She's a very cheerful person, and she understands my problems because her father is what she calls 'a recovered alcoholic'. We help each other out with things. I baby-sit for her daughter who only lives round the corner from me, and she's going to go with me the next time I visit my own daughter in hospital.

Your supporter

You *should* try to talk to people you trust about the way in which alcohol is affecting your partner. Of course there will be a limit to how much you want to tell people, but 'speaking out' about how the drinking is affecting your life, and talking about what you are doing to improve things should help to strengthen your resolve and to rid you of pent-up feelings of frustration.

There is another step that you can take which should make your attempts to improve things far easier. It involves asking a close and dependable friend or relative to help you with the things mentioned in this book. By the time you've finished this chapter, you will have decided all the important things you want to do.

A friend or relative (your 'supporter') can be asked to read through the decisions you've recorded on the worksheets. You want to know how they feel they can help you to carry your decisions through. For example, at the end of the last chapter, you drew up your own personal contract for 'Taking Action on Drinking'. One useful way in which your supporter can help is by checking over this page with you every week to judge your progress and to help with any difficulties you may have. You may decide it's a good idea for your supporter to read the entire book.

Ian broke down one morning during a visit from his brother-in-law, Alec. His girlfriend, Janet, had not come home from a night out, at a girlfriend's house, and he ended by telling Alec all about Janet's drinking, and about how she was putting him down continually in front of other people. Alec asked him what he was doing to cope with it all, and Ian showed him this book, knowing that Alec was someone he could trust.

IAN:

I'd read the part about finding a 'supporter', and Alec came to mind straight away. It seemed right to talk to him and ask for help, but I'd held back from talking to anyone else because I suppose part of me felt the things Janet was saying about me were true. Alec had only been in the house a few minutes before I poured out everything. He's promised to help a lot. He says he doesn't want to help by just giving sympathy, although he does seem to understand my problems. What he wants to do is to help in practical ways so that I can try and change things and make the right decisions.

A word of caution, though. It can be damaging rather than helpful to you if your supporter tries to force decisions upon you. Avoid anyone who is likely to do this. The person to make decisions about your life has to be you. But your chief supporter can help you to arrive at the *best* decisions. He or she can check your approach to decision-making and problem-solving by working through the section on pages 107–18 with you.

Taking action on friendship

The first steps are often the hardest. On the next work-sheet (page 96) there are some examples of how to begin. Start by completing the itemised things which you think will be most beneficial to you. Then turn back to the diary sheets on pages 85–6 and work from the 'Friendship list' now in the same way that you worked from your 'Activity list' before. Write down your plans for putting this new list into practice, but do remember to refer back to your 'diary' regularly, to refresh your memory regarding these plans.

3. Dealing with depression

GRAHAM:

Once I'd seen the counsellor about Susan's drinking, I knew she had a genuine alcohol problem and I should do something – about the drinking and driving especially. But I just didn't seem to be able to carry out any of the advice. All I wanted to do was forget about it all, and most nights I'd just end up doing nothing, just smoking one cigarette after another in front of the TV.

I found it more and more difficult to get up in the mornings because everything seemed such an effort, and there seemed nothing worth getting up for. I wanted to turn the clock back, or swap my life with someone else's. All the things that used to matter to me didn't have any meaning for me at all any more.

Then I wondered if there was something physically wrong with me because I couldn't sleep well and people at work noticed I'd lost weight. Also I felt tired all the time. I went to the doctor who asked a lot of questions, and diagnosed depression. He started me on a course of tablets, but warned me it would be a few weeks before they began to help me. I've got to go back and see him.

FRIENDSHIP LIST

1. **Renew contact with —————— and —————— by phone or letter.**

2. **Stop and chat to my neighbour ——————the next time we bump into each other.**

3. **Write a letter to ——————.**

4. **Ask —————— if I (and the children) can come and stay for a few days.**

5. **Decide whether to ask ———————, or —————— to be my chief supporter.**

6. **Contact and arrange to meet with my chief supporter.**

7. **Arrange to meet up with ——————.**

8. **Think of somewhere to go or to join where I am likely to meet new people.**

9.

10.

11.

12.

13.

14.

15.

Now go to page 84 to complete the diary sheets.

In Chapter 1 we looked at some of the negative feelings the partners of problem drinkers have, and tried to make sense of how they originate. In the next two sections we go a step further and suggest how to cope with depression and anxiety. Useful books and addresses are listed on pages 162–3 if you would like to seek extra help. However all the items we have discussed so far, including thinking positively about yourself, keeping contact with friends and relations and finding things to enjoy, add up to an excellent plan for keeping depression and anxiety at bay.

Depression is quite different from being unhappy. The following list is a sample of the various ways in which people suffering from depression have been known to describe their illness:

- Feeling cut off from everyone and everything – even oneself.
- A sense of total failure.
- Poor appetite and interrupted sleeping patterns.
- Feeling exhausted all the time.
- Little interest in personal appearance.
- No interest in doing anything.
- No enthusiasm for anything.
- Feeling life is meaningless.
- Feeling totally helpless to change anything.

If you think you are depressed, you must see your doctor. He may prescribe drugs to help you get through this initial period of time. After you have seen your doctor try the following suggestions:

First: be kind to yourself
Look closely at what you expect of yourself.

- Do you set unrealistically high standards for yourself and castigate yourself with vicious self-criticism each time you fall short?
- Do you want everyone to like and respect you?
- Do you keep on comparing yourself to other people, and always look for proof that they are better than you?
- Are you frightened to be close to other people because you feel they will reject you when they discover your faults?

SONIA:

I suppose I've always had a low opinion of myself, and it got a lot worse since Clive became a really heavy drinker. Other people seemed more interesting and more capable than me, and I always felt my own failings were somehow to blame for Clive's drinking. The fact that he used to criticise me a lot certainly didn't help matters. My older son goes out drinking with Clive a lot now, and sometimes he backs his Dad up when he starts criticising me.

I've put on quite a lot of weight over the past two years, and though I could afford it I don't think I deserve any new clothes until I've managed to go on a diet. Yesterday I noticed a vacancy for a part-time saleswoman in a dress shop round the corner, but I don't think they'd feel I was smart or capable enough. Anyway I'm feeling very tired these days, and don't like going out much.

If you are similarly self-critical, try to stop punishing yourself. People who victimise themselves in this way are bound to get depressed in the long run. Instead of tearing yourself apart, make allowances for yourself as you would do for others. Forgive yourself for mistakes, praise yourself for trying to tackle difficult problems, be patient with yourself when you are struggling with a solution and be kind to yourself.

Many people feel that to be positive about themselves amounts to being arrogant or boastful. They consider modesty and self-sacrifice to be essential virtues, and feel that even to talk about themselves is a form of conceit. If you are anything like this there is room to build your image up. It might be useful to turn back to the section on page 14. Check to see if you still think negatively about yourself. It is most important that you learn to think and talk positively. The next worksheet (see page 101) suggests good and bad ways to react as things happen to you. Write down, for your own use, some positive reactions to the last items on the list.

Second: force yourself to be active
Fight against apathy, against not wanting to do things. Start with easy activities, like those suggested below. Add your own ideas to the list, and do one each day. It is important that you work through all the sections in this chapter, particularly the section called 'Finding things to enjoy'.

Soak in a hot bath
Have a pleasant walk
Play with pets
Take up a hobby
Go to the cinema
Read your favourite magazine

Phone a special friend
Listen to music
Window shop
Watch a TV programme

Third: learn to stand up for yourself.
Don't put up with unfair criticism, and burden yourself
with guilt. Guilt and bottled up feelings can lead to
depression. Cope with anger in the way we suggested
on pages 15–17. Remember you have the right to say
'No', to refuse a request, and you have the right to
express your own viewpoint.

Finally: don't get depressed about depression.
Remind yourself of times when you felt better, and
understand that you can feel better again. Talking to
people you trust, having their help when you do the
things suggested here should make you feel better. Be
kind to yourself, be patient about your rate of progress,
but be firm in your intention to become more active.
Ask your supporter for help.

THINGS THAT HAPPEN: HOW YOU REACT

Example: You are criticised for a mistake you made at work.

Bad Reaction: 'That just goes to show how careless I can be'.

Good Reaction: 'I must work out how to avoid that in future – but it was an easy mistake to make'.

Example: You lose your temper with your daughter for breaking a favourite ornament.

Bad Reaction: 'Most other parents wouldn't let themselves rant and rave like this'.

Good Reaction: 'I don't often lose my temper. I'm only human like anyone else'.

Example: A close friend never returned a phone call.

Bad Reaction: 'Jane can't be interested in me any more'.

Good Reaction:

Example: Feeling anxious all day and not being able to concentrate on anything.

Bad Reaction: 'I never feel on top of things and always let my worries get the better of me'.

Good Reaction:

4. Coping with anxiety

Caroline is in her early fifties. Her husband used to be the skipper of a fishing boat, but now he is retired. He has no interests and spends most of his time drinking. The children have all left home, and Caroline feels trapped.

I've always respected Bill, although we were never close. He's always worked hard, but has never been involved much with the family – he was never at home much. I've led a life of my own bringing up the children, and I do a lot of sewing and gardening.

I've tried everything I can think of to stop Bill's drinking, but nothing seems to work. His whole life seems to revolve around it, and I'm frightened about his health. Yesterday he fell down the steps, but he didn't hurt himself. I've got tied to the house because I feel I can't trust him. I feel panicky all the time. I can't concentrate or relax. The smallest thing is hard to do, and I get upset and sometimes tearful very easily. If I go into the garden I often get a gripping sensation in my throat, start sweating, and imagine something dreadful is going to happen. Going shopping is just a nightmare. If I can I get my daughter to bring it in for me.

Everyone feels anxious and tense some of the time. Tension helps to keep us alert so we can react swiftly to dangerous situations. We all have a built in warning system which enables us to decide whether to fight or run from a real threat or challenge. It involves body changes. Adrenalin and various hormones enter the bloodstream and are pumped all round the body. Our heart and breathing rates increase. We sweat and become tense and panicky.

Many people do not need to be exposed to a real threat or challenge for their bodies to produce a state of anxiety or panic. Their panic attacks and anxiety states are provoked by their own disturbing imaginary fears, by practical worries and stress. Tension and panic build up as they imagine problems they feel unable to cope with. When life seems threatening all the time, our built-in alarm systems remain permanently switched on. The kind of anxiety symptoms this provokes are:

- Stiffness, aches, and pains in the back, chest, neck and jaw
- Headaches and indigestion
- Butterflies in the stomach
- Palpitations in the chest
- Pins and needles in extremities (arms, hands, legs, feet)
- Tightness in the throat
- Irritability and jumpiness
- Feelings of fear or panic towards situations, or objects
- Forebodings and premonitions that terrible things are about to happen.

If you suffer from these symptoms, how can you deal with them?

First of all, understand them for what they are
Don't try to fight these feelings by tensing up. Accept

the anxiety in the sure knowledge that it will fade eventually. Let it wash over you but, as it does, keep reminding yourself why this is happening, and continue to work your way through the second and third steps.

Second, analyse your thoughts
As you begin to feel the familiar stirrings of anxiety, force yourself to think positively. Tell yourself 'I *can* cope', 'We all make mistakes sometimes', or whatever you might say to another person in the same circumstance of suffering from fear and anxiety. Nip your negative thoughts in the bud, and replace them with kinder, more constructive ideas.

Be sure to do the work on pages 13–15, as it will help you to prevent anxiety from building up.

Finally, learn to relax
When you feel anxious, you are physically tense too. Coax yourself to relax. This will also help the tension to melt away. Relaxation, however, takes practice. You need to relax your mind as well as your body. The worksheet suggests how to go about this but it is important to find a quiet time and place and to give yourself at least half an hour to work the exercise through. Once you've mastered relaxing in a quiet place you'll be able to practice relaxing wherever you are. As soon as you feel anxiety or panic rising inside you, just remember these rules:

— Breathe slowly . . .
— Understand what is going on . . .
— Loosen up your muscles and . . .
— Calm your thoughts.
— Think of the letters BULC as soon as anxiety starts to take hold of you.

Janet first started getting into what her doctor called 'anxiety attacks' when her husband went to prison for his part in a drunken brawl. Although he has no recollection of what happened, he was found guilty of serious assault.

It was a very bad time for me, looking after three children, with hardly any money coming in. A lot of people turned away from me and the family, but other people really tried to help a lot. But while Norman was 'inside' I ended up getting hooked on the tranquillisers my doctor gave me to cope with my anxiety states. After being on them for nearly a year I was like a zombie, not feeling part of life any more, not able to make decisions and still suffering from anxiety. Trying to cut down made me much worse.

When Norman was released he saw a difference in me straight away. He'd taken part in a drug education programme in prison, and knew all about addiction to pills like tranquillisers. We talked and eventually agreed to tell my doctor I was joining a tranquilliser self help group to help me wean myself off the pills. I've managed it and learned a lot about how to relax and keep the anxiety at bay. It hasn't been easy, but Norman's given me a lot of encouragement. I suppose he felt responsible in a way.

Since coming out of prison he hasn't been drinking at all, and has steered clear of his old mates. He got a lot of help from a social worker while in prison, and started seeing an alcohol counsellor before he was released. He's a lot more involved with the children now, but depressed about losing his job.

RELAXATION EXERCISE

Step 1 Sit down in a very quiet place, and close your eyes.

Step 2 Tell yourself you aim to feel peaceful and calm.

Step 3 Start to slow down your breathing. Let your stomach and chest expand as you breathe in through your nose and fall as your breathe out through your mouth.

Step 4 Work through all the different muscles in your body tensing each one up in turn and then relaxing it. As you relax tell that part of your body to grow heavy and loose.

Step 5 Allow your entire body to feel heavy and loose, and keep on with the deep breathing.

Step 6 Attempt to free your mind of any thought at all. Thinking of a nice scene – like blue sky, or a deserted beach – might help.

Step 7 Repeat the 'relaxation word' **BULC**, *once* as you breathe in, and *again* as you breathe out. Keep doing this. If you find your thoughts drifting, bring them back to concentrating on this one word.

Step 8 Repeat the last 3 steps until you feel pleasantly relaxed. Continue for a further 5 minutes or so – then *slowly* open your eyes and rest quietly for a few minutes.

If you find your mind wandering, remember that you WILL get better with practice.

LEARNING WHAT'S BEST FOR YOURSELF

If you are now beginning to do more in your spare time, and are making contact with other people, you are probably worrying less about your partner's drinking, and thinking a little more about yourself and your own needs.

This chapter discusses how to get more out of life for yourself – in spite of your partner's drinking problems. Meanwhile, with your supporter's help you have started to put into practice your personal contract on 'Acting on Drinking'. To carry through these plans you may want to improve two particular skills which will make your efforts easier, by increasing your confidence in your ability to change things.

These skills are learning techniques in how to make decisions, and how to solve problems. People who have mastered them have a greater sense of being in control of their own lives.

1. Making decisions

People make decisions in different ways. Some people rely mainly on their feelings, hunches or intuitions. Others weigh up the pros and cons of different actions or meticulously plan a strategy. It may take a long time to think through one decision, while you may easily arrive at another. Sometimes people wait until others decide for them, or 'drift' until circumstances decide.

HARRY:

Trying to work out how to cope with Ann's drinking has made me see that I've let her make all the decisions in our marriage. I'm easygoing, and I've just wanted to have a quiet life. But then I thought that through not standing up to Ann's drinking, I wasn't helping either of us. I was losing respect for myself, and all the time the drinking was getting worse. I knew I had to take some action on the drinking, and I'd begun to realise I should start having the courage to leave Ann on her own sometimes and put some things back into my life. I think first of all though, I have to learn to start talking to Ann again – about the things that matter to us.

Given the situation you're in, you could be faced with making some very difficult decisions, to do with the welfare of your entire family. There may be special religious or moral viewpoints which come into your decisions.

The next 2 worksheets set out the different stages you must go through to reach a well thought out decision. We have set down an example, to show you how to think through these stages. Whenever you are faced with a serious or difficult decision you can turn back to these pages for help.

2. Solving problems

Problems may be of our own making, or be forced upon us. Whatever their source, we may soon feel uncomfortably anxious, and helpless in the face of them. Sharing the way you feel with your chief supporter can help, but it is important that *you* are the one who can work out what is best for you.

(Continued on page 113.)

DECISION-MAKING STAGES

1. Write down what it is you need to decide about.
   e.g. How to spend our holidays

2. Why does this decision matter so much? Write it down.
   Worries e.g. about how John will behave – how much he will drink. Can we afford to go away?

3. Write down what you need to find out first of all to help you make your decision.
   e.g. How do the children feel – what do they want? Could Jack and Joan 'cope' with John if we went away together? What would a caravan holiday cost? Would Jack and Joan understand we have less money to spend? How much money could we set aside?

4. Make a note of the different decisions you could make and of the good and bad things each decision could lead to.

Decision	Good Results	Bad Results
(a) Stay at home	(i) Save money.	(i) Children bored and resentful.
	(ii) Time to do things in the house.	(ii) I wouldn't get a break.
	(iii) Could have day trips.	(iii) John might spend the holiday money on drink.
	(iv) No embarrassing holiday incidents.	

(b) All of us go away on a cheap holiday with Jack and Joan.

(i) Keep a better eye on the drinking.
(ii) Alternative adult company for me.
(iii) John may drink less.

(i) Could be more than we can afford.

(c) Go away for a few days just with the children.

(i) Very relaxing for me.
(ii) Less stressful for the children.
(iii) Would cost less.

(i) John could be angry at being left out.
(ii) John might cause trouble at home.
(iii) I might worry.

5. Circle your *best* choice: (a), (b) or (c).

6. Make a note of what you need to do to carry this through.
   (a) Talk things over with Jack and Joan. (b) Check costs. (c) Make sure I'm holding the purse strings.

Decision-Making Stages

1. Write down what it is you need to decide about.

2. Why does this decision matter so much? Write it down.

3. Write down what you need to find out to help you make your decision.

4. Make a note of the different decisions you can make and the good or bad things each decision can lead to.

Decision   *Good Results*   *Bad Results*

(a)

(b)

(c)

5. Circle your *best* choice: (a), (b) or (c).

6. Make a note of what you need to do to carry this through.

Caroline is worried about her daughter, whose baby is due in two months.

> I would like to go and look after my daughter Catherine's two children while she's in hospital having the baby. My son-in-law has been ill with angina and I know he'd value the help. But I'm worried about the panic attacks starting up again, although I seem to have got them under control. Most of all I'm worried about leaving Bill at home on his own when he's drinking so much. Catherine's got a friend who might be able to help, and then I could always see if my sister could go and stay. I can't think about it without getting worked up, and I don't think Catherine wants to ask me in case I feel I can't cope.

It can help to learn the stages in problem solving by first of all practising on someone else's problem. Imagine, for example, that a friend comes to *you* with the problem of being seriously in debt.

First of all you would probably encourage your friend to calm down and put him or her into a frame of mind where he or she can think more clearly about the situation.

Next, you would try to find out what it is about his or her debts that is most worrying. For example, maybe she has received 2 threatening letters from creditors, or dreads having to tell his or her partner.

Then, you would want to work out, with your friend what might be done to lessen the problem – for example he or she might see a social worker, borrow more money, come to an arrangement with the worst creditor, try to earn extra money, sell something or, if possible, cut down expenditures. In weighing up the alternatives, your friend must consider all the pros and cons of each.

Finally you would help him or her to choose one or more of the possibilities, and to work out and carry through a plan of action.

In helping your friend with his or her problem, you have worked through five stages. These stages are laid out in the next worksheet (page 115). To practice applying problem solving skills to your own problems, go back to page 82 and reconsider the 2 things you thought you would like to spend time doing, if only they weren't impossible. Write the least difficult of these 2 at the top of the first worksheet – there is an example to help you – then go on to work through the various problem solving stages, just to see how readily you can come up with a solution to a problem which seemed impossible to solve.

Finally turn over and repeat the exercise with the second problem.

PROBLEM SOLVING EXERCISE – PROBLEM I

Sample Problem: I can't go climbing because there's no one to look after the baby.

Your Problem:

Step I	Try to think objectively about the problem by imagining that it is someone else's problem and he or she is asking your advice.
Step II	What concerns you most? Write down the most worrying aspects of the problem.
Step III	Write down as many ways you can think of to solve the problem, or to make things better at least.

1

2

3

4

5

6

Step IV   Write down the pros and cons of the 3 most
realistic solutions:
Pro   *Con*
1

2

3

Step V   Choose and write down the best solution(s).
Describe how you hope to carry it (them)
through.

PROBLEM SOLVING EXERCISE – PROBLEM 2

Your Problem:

Step I   Try to think objectively about the problem
by imagining it is someone else's, and he or
she is asking for your help.

Step II   What concerns you most? Write down the
most worrying aspects of the problem.

Step III   Write down as many ways you can think of
to solve the problem, or make things better
at least.

1

2

3

4

5

6

Step IV Write down the pros and cons of the 3 most
realistic solutions:
   Pro   *Con*

1

2

3

Step V Choose and write down the best solution(s).
Describe how you hope to carry it (them)
through.

MAKING PLANS FOR THE FUTURE

If you are living with a drinker, and his or her drinking
problem is severe, reading this book may be your last
attempt to try and change things. You may have set a
time limit for things to improve. Or you may have
decided – perhaps even told your partner – that if
things ever get really bad again, you would walk out
altogether.

Perhaps you have not been thinking along these lines, but you do, nevertheless, find it difficult to keep anxiety at bay as you agonise over such questions as, 'What do I do if *this* happens?' . . . 'How do I cope if that happens?' . . . Your fears may revolve around the subject of financial ruin, physical abuse, or accidental fire. They may have a basis in your real experience or be 'worst scenario' fantasies – whichever they are they cannot be ignored because they worry you.

Trial separations

You may have tried to separate from your partner for a brief time already and taken your children with you. This may have worked as a 'cooling-down' period, and brought hope that your partner would agree to control his or her drinking. Perhaps friends or relatives are able to help you out from time to time.

If so, deciding to separate for a while and to come back together only if or when the drinker shows that he is taking positive action about drinking, could become a clause in your contract with yourself (see page 64). You can choose to separate in order to put pressure on your partner, even if no one in the family is seriously in danger of being hurt.

On the other hand, you may feel obliged to separate to protect someone in the family who is being hurt or abused. This still counts as an opportunity to put press-ure on your partner about drinking, and permits you to dictate the terms under which you are willing to reunite. Studying the contents of pages 66–73 again may shed some light on this. Above all, once you have reached an agreement, you must stick to it or your partner will not take you seriously and the problems will certainly recur.

IAN:

Alec (my supporter) and I worked out a number of things I could do to put pressure on Janet about her drinking. Although she drank less, her attitude to me when she was drinking didn't seem to change. I never managed to get her to talk openly either about the drinking or about the relationship. In the end I arranged to stay with George at work, telling Janet I'd be back only if she'd see someone about her drinking. I'd seen a lawyer beforehand who assured me that because we didn't have children I would not lose any rights to the house by doing this. I'm still fond of Janet but the drinking had got right in the way of having a decent relationship. I'm just hoping that now she'll start to think seriously about it all.

If you feel that a trial separation could be useful to you try to plan ahead for it. The actual decision of when to go may have to be made on the spot, but you can work out long in advance what circumstances are likely to force the issue. For example, being locked out yet again might be your personal trigger mechanism.

There are other things you could plan ahead for which would make separating safer and smoother. This could involve speaking to a lawyer about your rights and to a social worker about financial assistance. You could find out what moral and material support you would be able to get from friends. Certainly you would need to know where you could stay, if for some reason it were to prove impossible for your partner to stay elsewhere.

It might also help to store some money and clothing

in a safe place. Finally, you may want to set time aside to talk to your children to prepare them for the possibility of a trial separation.

Your worst fears
It is natural and inevitable that from time to time you will fear the worst. This does not mean that you are giving up hope. It means only that, at the moment, you have reached a low ebb. Even so, it would be misleading to suggest that no crisis will ever occur. Some minor crisis – like being locked out of the house – is almost bound to happen, and quite probably you have imagined far worse. The worst may never come to pass but it is important that you be honest with yourself and face up to your fears.

Find a piece of paper and write down ALL the things you fear. Then pick 3 items from your list – after some thought cross off whatever fears seem unlikely or manageable. Now take another piece of paper and write down all the things you can do if any of these terrible things did come to pass. In doing this remember what you learned from the problem-solving section on page 108.

You might, for example, be worried about what to do the next time your husband causes a disturbance by coming home so drunk in the early hours of the morning. Maybe you are afraid that the neighbours will call the police. After writing down all the ways you've tried to cope in the past, and after thinking up several new options, you end up choosing the plan below:

(1) Tell Steve, the next time you confront him about his drinking, that if he and the boys ever

turn up drunk in the early hours again, you will go away for a few days with the children.

(2) Ask a close friend or family member to be ready to put you up for a few days in an emergency.

(3) Have ready a supply of clothes and cash in case you should have to leave home in an emergency.

Now, find three pieces of paper and write down your plans for the 3 possible crises in your life that you feel you should prepare for. Remember to note down all the ways of coping you can think of before deciding which plan is best for you. Keep these 3 pieces of paper hidden in a very safe place so that whenever you feel worried about coping, you can check them over to reassure yourself about your plans.

SUMMARY: HOW YOU PLAN TO COPE

This chapter has covered a lot of ground and required hard work. To recheck the things you plan to do, tick the boxes below as they apply. Allow yourself several weeks to carry things through. Inevitably, you will have difficulty with some things, but the final chapter should help you to overcome these difficulties.

Enjoying my spare time
(1) 3 things to do more often ☐
(2) 3 things to start now ☐
(3) 3 things to do later ☐
(4) Keep my Activity Diary up to date ☐

Building good relationships
(1) Find a supporter ☐
(2) Take first steps towards friendship ☐
(3) Keep my Friendship Diary up to date ☐

Dealing with depression
(1) See my doctor ☐
(2) Learn to think positively ☐
(3) Force activity upon myself ☐
(4) Learn to stand up for myself ☐

Coping with anxiety
(1) Learn positive thinking ☐
(2) Learn to relax ☐
(3) Understand how anxiety builds up ☐

Solving problems
(1) Learn the problem-solving method by resolving problems about things I feel are impossible for me to do ☐

Making decisions
(1) Learn the decision-making steps ☐

Planning for the future
(1) Decide how to deal with my worst fears ☐
(2) Talk to my supporter about trial separations ☐

(3) Talk to my children about possible emergencies and/or
separations ☐

6

YOUR
CHILDREN

If you have children you have probably wondered how the drinking problem may be affecting or harming them, and how you can give them moral support. This chapter will help you work out what to do, and also suggests ways of coping with other especially tricky situations. There are some guidelines on page 134 to help children 12 years old or over.

Janice is 11 and feels very mixed up. She wonders why her mother isn't like other mothers, why she sleeps all day long and never seems to care any more about anyone or anything. She can't understand why her father is always bad tempered and angry with everyone.

Janice's father expects her to prepare the evening meal and to keep things clean and tidy. She is also expected to keep an eye on her younger brother. Her father washes and irons the clothes and does most of the shopping, but Janice knows it won't be long before she is expected to do this too.

When my mother disappears for a few days I sometimes wish that she would never come back, or get knocked down and killed by a car. Then I feel angry at myself for having such wicked thoughts, and wonder if my mother's drinking is all because of me. I wish I could talk to my best friend Susie, but she's moved away and I daren't ask another friend home in case my mother's drunk.

This is just one example of how a child might see things. Naturally, every child's experience is different, but children can be affected and hurt in much the same way as partners. The things that hurt children most are:

- Not being able to depend on parents to provide necessities and to keep promises.
- Feeling confused and uncertain of what may happen next.
- Being unable to cope with school work because of worry and tiredness.
- Sensing a bad atmosphere at home, finding themselves involved in family fights and squabbles, or being kept awake by them.
- Feeling they can't talk to their sober parent because he or she is always irritable, nagging or exhausted.
- Wondering if *they* are the cause of their parent's drinking, or if their other parent, who nags and shouts continually, may be at fault.
- Losing friends and interests.
- Resentment at having to take on adult responsibilities.
- Fear of being hurt.

WHAT CHILDREN NEED

Children *can* cope when their parent drinks too much. In fact, some children become very capable as a direct result. But so much depends on how their other parent copes with the drinking problem, however bad it may be.

Your children have the same need as other people's children for love, warmth, kindness, and firmness. They need a predictable routine of regular meals, bedtimes, and special occasions to celebrate like birthdays. They need to feel wanted, and to be protected from at least some of the crises and responsibilities of the adult world.

They have a right to be heard and to be taken seriously, and they need to have free time for play, friends and outside interests. Above all, no one has the right to abuse a child, physically or emotionally.

PAT:

I noticed that as Jack's drinking was getting worse, my two older children, aged 14 and 16, were spending more and more of their spare time away from home.

After a while I challenged them about this and they said they couldn't stand being in the house when their father was drunk. Another problem seemed to be *me* – they saw me as picking on them all the time, and not showing any interest in the things they were doing. I felt angry about their attitude, but at least we started talking about the drinking and began to understand each other's feelings a bit better.

YOUR OWN CHILDREN

There are some important but quite easy ways in which you can help your children to cope. Of course the kind of help you give them, and the way you give it depends on their age. You can help a great deal by:

1. *Talking to them about the drinking problem.*
Go over with them the basic things that you have learned about alcohol from Chapters 2 and 3. Emphasise that the strange behaviour their other parent sometimes exhibits towards them is caused by drinking. Point out that they are very much loved by *both* parents and find evidence to prove this.

2. *Explaining they are not responsible.*
Children need to know that problems at home are not their fault and that there is nothing they have done to feel guilty about. Explain that there is little they can do directly to influence the drinking problem, although you are *trying* to change things. Point out, honestly, that they will probably have to cope with the problem for some time to come.

3. *Showing how you feel about things.*
Sometimes you will be too impatient, tired or caught up in problems to be responsive to your children in the way they need and want. You may speak and behave towards them in ways that you later regret. It helps if children understand that you are not indifferent towards them but are overwhelmed by all sorts of difficulties; many of which have been caused by the drinking, and

have left you tense and preoccupied. So explain, as simply as you can, why you sometimes behave inadequately, and ask them to be patient and understanding with you.

4. *Allowing them their childhood*.
Just like you, your children need to organise their lives so that good things can happen to them in spite of the drinking problem. This means encouraging them to keep up, or start up, friendships and interests. It also means being firm with yourself about not giving them too many adult responsibilities. Children should help at home of course – but not at the expense of their childhood. They need play and friendships to develop into mentally and physically healthy adults.

As Margaret saw less and less of her friends and family, she grew much closer to her children, a daughter aged 12 and a son aged 14. She confided in them about her worries about their father, and they comforted her when she got upset.

I learned to rely a lot on the children to buck me up when things got bad. They helped a lot around the house and I felt proud about how grown up they were in their attitude. Then I got resentful the times they wanted to go out and be with their friends. Now I realise I was expecting too much of them and I should have turned to my own friends for moral support.

PREPARING CHILDREN FOR EMERGENCIES

You don't want to frighten your children by letting their imagination run riot about all the traumatic things that might be caused by your partner's drinking. On the other hand, you would feel more in control of the situation, and they would be more confident, if you could decide well in advance how to deal with dangerous events should they arise.

Here are some examples you might want to consider speaking about with your children. After all, children *should* know how to cope in an emergency, whether or not their parent drinks too much.

Drinking and driving

No one should travel in a car when the driver has been drinking, so ask your children to think of ways to avoid that. Perhaps someone else can be persuaded to drive or other ways can be found to get wherever they are going. Maybe they can stay with a friend, provided you know where they are. Even a decision *not* to depend on the drinker for a lift would help.

Sudden illness

If drinking stops suddenly the drinker may become severely ill, experiencing withdrawal symptoms, including vomiting and fits. This is always a risk, and there are other everyday risks too, like injuries from falls or burns, which may need quick medical attention. Your child should know how, and under what circumstances, to call a doctor or an ambulance.

Fire

There is always a risk of fire in the home. Since fires are commonly caused by flaming chip pans and by smoking, the risk of fire is increased when the person cooking or smoking is drunk. Your children should be told to leave the house instantly in the event of a fire, and to call for help and the fire brigade from outside the house. They should know that they can suffocate in a few minutes and that this is an even greater danger than burning to death. For this reason it is dangerous to stop even to rescue an animal or favourite toy.

Being manipulated

Your partner might be tempted to use the children for protection, asking them to cover up, tell lies and do other dishonest things. You can discourage this by talking about this problem openly from every angle with your children, and by teaching them how to say 'No', politely but firmly.

Abuse

It does not follow that children who come from homes where a parent drinks too much are necessarily physically injured or sexually abused, but it *can* happen. More often children are taunted, ignored, humiliated or ridiculed, which is damaging enough. If *you* are being physically abused by the drinker, however, there is a strong possibility that your child is being abused, too, or may be at risk. If this danger exists, you must let your children know that they can talk to you about anything at any time. You must make it clear that you want to know and will protect them. Children are often too frightened to tell anyone about abuse and assault. They may have been warned not to tell by the parent concerned, and may even have been threatened. Or, they may feel that they have to protect the parent from getting into trouble with you or the authorities. If you discover that your child is being abused, you must do all that you can to protect him or her.

The first step might be to contact an organisation which specialises in abuse problems. These organisations are listed on pages 156–7. If, however, you feel the need to go away somewhere safe with the children for a while before deciding what steps to take, the next chapter should help you to examine this option carefully. In either case, talk to someone straight away as it is intolerable to have to bear this fearful burden entirely alone.

SUMMARY

If your children are being harmed, however great or small the damage to them, there are several important steps you can take to give them the support they need. You can:

1. Help them to feel that you and your partner love and want them and that you do listen to them.
2. Talk to them about the drinking.
3. Explain that the drinking is not their fault in any way.
4. Show them how you feel.
5. Encourage them to play, see friends and explore their interests.

6. Resist burdening them with too many responsibilities.
7. Prepare them to be able to cope with hazards and dangers.
8. Make sure they trust you enough to tell you if they are being abused.

Try and decide now where you want to make a start. Keep referring back to the list, and tick off each item as you begin to work on it. If some things seem difficult, talk to your supporter about them. Don't feel you have to tackle everything at once.

You may find it useful to show your child the following guidelines but he or she will probably have to be at least 12 years old in order to understand them fully.

GUIDELINES FOR CHILDREN

When someone has a drinking problem, they are not the only one who gets hurt. Drinking causes problems for everyone and it can make friends and family as unhappy as it makes the drinker.

People who have a drinking problem often let drink run their lives. Alcohol makes them forget even the feelings of the people they love, and they don't always realise that their drinking is upsetting the family.

How do you know if someone is drinking too much?

You can usually tell when someone is drinking too much. They may get drunk in the house. They may become angry or violent after drinking too much, and there may be lots of family fights. But some people try to hide the fact that they are drinking too much. They sometimes hide their bottles in strange places, or make up excuses for themselves.

If you have a parent who drinks too much you may begin to notice that:

- Promises may not be kept.
- Your parent may act strangely or have funny moods.
- You may smell alcohol on your parent's breath.
- There may be times when he or she goes off alone, and gets drunk.
- Family life will change.
- Meals may not get made or they may be broken off suddenly.
- Things which have to be done may not be done.

- Your parent's moods may change so quickly that you will sometimes wonder where you stand.
- There may not be enough money to go around.

How do you feel?

If one of your parents has a drinking problem, you may not know what to do a lot of the time.

You may feel *scared and mixed-up*, wondering what will happen next.

You are bound to feel *angry and embarrassed* because of the way the drinker often behaves, especially if your parent lets you down or breaks promises.

You may even feel *angry with yourself* for not being able to change things, or you may feel *guilty* because you imagine that somehow it is your fault that your parent drinks too much.

All these bad feelings are hard to live with. They make it hard to concentrate. To keep things going at home you may end up sometimes trying to do things like housework yourself, even when this means taking time off schoolwork or playtime.

Perhaps you also try to hide things from relatives and neighbours in order to protect your parent, and you may pretend to yourself that these problems don't really exist, or will soon go away. You may have started to feel very lonely and different from your friends and other children, and you may also feel that you no longer have a life of your own. And, on top of all this, your non-drinking parent may seem to be nagging you all the time.

What you can do

If there is somebody in your family whose drinking is causing problems, the most important thing to do is to work out a way to keep life as normal as possible.

People with drinking problems cannot change their habits quickly. You may have to live with your parent's problem for a long time. If you can accept that fact it will start to get easier to deal with the problems that drinking causes.

Don't try to lecture your father or mother about his or her drinking. There may be times when it is possible for you to talk to him or her in an easy, friendly way about drinking and then if you want to, you can describe how much drinking is hurting the family and how upset it makes you. This may help your parent to realise that it is time for him or her to get help, but don't nag or push things too far, too quickly.

Try to be understanding and help your other parent. That parent, like you, has all sorts of problems to deal with because of the drinking.

Steps to take

FIRST, find out all about alcohol
Learn as much as you can. You can phone up for some leaflets from a local alcohol advice centre. Look in a 'phone book under **Alcohol.**

Don't try to find out though by drinking yourself. That won't help to solve the difficulties you have. It would only cause more problems, because you would lose control, too.

SECOND, talk to someone you trust

It helps to share a problem and people who care for you – friends, relatives, teachers or neighbours – have probably guessed that something is wrong and would like to help you.

THIRD, don't blame yourself

You are not to blame for the problems in your family. Your parents don't do bad things because of you, or because they don't love you. They can make mistakes and do the wrong things in the same way children do.

You know when a grown-up is doing or asking you to do wrong things. Don't allow them to expect that of you NOT even if you feel very sorry for them. Even if your own parent asks you to keep a special secret or to do something you feel is wrong don't do it. That's the time to tell your other parent. You can also speak to someone trained to help people with drink problems and their families. This call can be confidential, just look in a 'phone book under **Alcohol**. You *must* speak to someone quickly.

FINALLY, make the best of your own life

Fill up your time enjoyably and try to forget about the drinking. There are interesting things going on outside your home that you can get involved in. Go to your local Sports or Community Centre and find out what's on. Perhaps there are ways that you can earn extra pocket money, too, like delivering newspapers and washing cars. Remember, you are not an adult, and you don't need to take on adult problems and tasks yet, so try to live your own life and enjoy things, in spite of the drinking problem in your family. People may pressure you to do what they want, but try to do what you think is right for you.

7

TAKING STOCK

Even if you have tried to work through all the parts of this book which interest you, you have probably found that you are able to make progress only in a few areas. It is not a good idea to expect instant progress. You have to be realistic and not expect too much, too soon.

However, if all you have done so far is simply to read this book *you are not ready for this chapter*. You need to work at putting all the practical suggestions into action for several weeks before getting any benefit from this chapter. Some of the changes you are trying to make can be achieved fairly easily and quickly – like renewing contact with friends. Others – like building up self confidence – are long-term projects. It is common to make progress in one area and then to slip back, or so it will seem. In fact, you have probably made far more progress than you imagine. You may be overlooking genuine achievements while dwelling on difficulties.

This chapter is meant to help you assess your real

progress and decide what steps to take about the problems that you cannot work out.

HAVE THINGS CHANGED?

Below is a list of areas and problems that were covered in earlier chapters. It will help you decide how much progress you are making.

(Circle one)

1.	How I feel.	Better	No Better	Worse
2.	How I deal with my partner's drinking.	Better	No Better	Worse
3.	How I enjoy my spare time.	Better	No Better	Worse
4.	My relationships.	Better	No Better	Worse
5.	My self-confidence.	Better	No Better	Worse
6.	Solving problems.	Better	No Better	Worse
7.	Making decisions.	Better	No Better	Worse
8.	Standing up for myself.	Better	No Better	Worse
9.	My own drinking.	Better	No Better	Worse
10.	My anxiety.	Better	No Better	Worse
11.	My depression.	Better	No Better	Worse
12.	Plans for the future.	Better	No Better	Worse
13.	Being able to depend on a supporter.	Better	No Better	Worse
14.	Practical domestic problems.	Better	No Better	Worse
15.	My children's welfare.	Better	No Better	Worse

There are many reasons why you may be having difficulty with some of the things you are tackling. For example:

● *Being too hasty.*
You may be expecting to see major changes in too short a time, so that what might count as progress for someone else counts as failure for you. Or you may have tried to do too much at once, and not worked on the exercises properly.

● *Changes in your life.*
You may have had some upheaval – become ill, suffered a bereavement, moved house, taken in an elderly relative – and consequently found it difficult to concentrate on the work in hand.

● *No back-up.*
People on whom you thought you could depend to help you may have let you down or drifted away.

● *Feeling bad.*
Your feelings of anxiety, depression and confusion may be stopping you from committing yourself to positive action.

● *This book doesn't suit you.*
Some people find that a book on personal problems is not as helpful as other therapy techniques. Or, this book may only apply to *some* of the problems you are anxious to work on.

● *Losing heart.*
Your partner's drinking and behaviour may be getting worse instead of better despite all your efforts.

Shirley was trying to change a number of things in her life in spite of her boyfriend's drinking. She was beginning to feel more positive and had managed to talk to Stewart about his drinking.

But then things went wrong. I got ill and had to have an operation. And a close friend who'd been helping me through things, began to let me down. After that I seemed to get depressed and despondent. I saw a counsellor in the end, and I've now joined a support group for partners. It's helped to make me feel less isolated. But I feel the book helped me to get started on things, and I'm still using it.

COPING WITH DIFFICULTIES

The good things that can follow from working through this book are worth waiting for. The important thing is *not to give up* when progress seems slow. Here are some things that can help:

- Write down on a sheet of paper all the areas/items to which you have answered 'no better' or 'worse'. Then copy down from the checklist in the last section, which 'difficulties' apply to each.
- Use this section to decide on what action you ought to be taking. For example, if you have no support or back-up you might decide to see a counsellor.
- Ask yourself which of the items are most urgent, and which, if any, can be shelved until later. The work in 'Coping with Life' is more important than anything else in the book: you can only begin to help your partner and/or children by helping yourself become a stronger and happier person.
- Set aside some quiet time each day to work on the manual, and give yourself a realistic time-scale within which to achieve each item.

1. *Being too hasty*
You may be someone who rushes at things. If so, try to slow yourself down. Take things one step at a time, and work on the most important things first. But if you are too hasty because the problems are so bad that you can barely cope,

this may mean you would do better working
through this book with the help of a counsellor.

2. *When changes occur in your life*
Sudden changes are bound to throw you off
course. They will rob you of time and energy,
and you may forget all about your resolutions.
But eventually you should be able to get back
on course. Don't allow yourself to lose hope just
because things have been at a standstill for a
while.

HARRY:

Out of the blue I was told by my manager that I'd
have to take early retirement. I was miserable for
the following six months until I left, and I felt
worse afterwards. Ann was very angry about it,
but she also showed some sympathy for the way I
was feeling. I seemed to slip back into the 'old
me' for a while, just ignoring the drinking, or
pretending it wasn't as bad.

I got a lump sum when I retired, and had it
invested. But then I got the idea of spending some
of it on a short holiday for us both – and Ann
agreed. We enjoyed ourselves, and Ann drank
very little – perhaps because there was a lot to do
and she was away from friends. We ended up
being able to talk a bit about the drinking, and
she admitted she felt a lot better when she was
drinking less. She's now getting help from her
doctor. I'm not taking it for granted that things
will change, but at least it's a start.

3. *No back-up*
Being isolated from people when you need help
is the worst thing that can happen. In order to
strengthen your resolve and make your efforts
easier, find a supporter. Reread page 93 and the
previous pages again. If there is no one you can
turn to, think about finding a counsellor and try
contacting one of the addresses on page 160.

4. *Feeling bad*
Bad feelings hold us back from tackling new
things. We have suggested ways to cope with bad
feelings on pages 8 and 95. If you have not
worked through these pages thoroughly as yet,
do that next. For the moment, put aside the
remaining parts of the book.

However, if you find that the book is not
helping you to approach your problems, turn to
another source of help (see page 155). Once any
method at all has helped you gain some control
over your feelings, you will be able to pick up on
the other problems you want to work on later.
But remember that, if depression is a problem
for you, you would be wise to keep in touch with
your doctor.

5. *This book doesn't suit you*
You may feel, in the end, that working from a
book is not a satisfactory way for you to
approach your problems. All the same give the
book a fair chance for a few months – and don't
give up too easily. You may simply need *extra*
help with certain items. But if you do need a
different kind of help the final chapter should tell

you where to find it. Some people benefit most from seeing a counsellor regularly; someone they can talk to in detail about their problems.

6. *Losing heart*
There may come a point when you feel that you cannot take any more, and you give up trying to influence your partner's drinking. Although you want to help, remember that the drinking is your *partner's* responsibility. If your partner persists, in spite of everything, look very carefully at what it is you want. Who is being harmed and to what extent? How long can it continue? The notes in the next section will help you analyse this difficult question.

YOUR FUTURE WITH YOUR PARTNER

The idea of 'a trial separation' was suggested at the end of chapter 5 (page 119) as something you might want to try. It is one way to put pressure on your partner to change. But in some cases separation eventually proves the only sensible long-term way to cope with the drinking problem. If you are contemplating the idea of long-term separation this section may help you to organise your thoughts.

Even if you are not very closely involved with the drinker – for example, if you are not living together – you may feel the time has come to take stock of the relationship. You may feel manipulated, that he is taking advantage of you and you feel utterly worn out. If so, you have a right to review the relationship which has no give and take, and where you are nearly always the loser.

When it comes to close friendships and relationships everyone's personal needs and values differ. Many people reject separation as a solution. Others refuse to be trapped in relationships which are devoid of affection or trust, while still others never take stock of relationships, simply taking them for granted, regardless of their quality.

CAROLINE:

In the end I went to stay with my daughter and helped with the children while she had the baby. I stayed on for quite a while, and my husband went down south to stay with his brother and family. My daughter doesn't know, but I've made friends with a man in the village. We're now very close, and he wants more from the relationship. I don't think I do, but it's helped me get my self-confidence back. The time apart has made me determined to challenge my husband about his drinking when I go home. I'm also thinking about phoning his brother to see if he'd be prepared to talk to him about the drinking.

There are no rules to tell you where you stand in all this, but there are techniques to help you make difficult choices.

Talk to people you trust

Get help from your 'supporter' and from others with whom you see eye to eye. Consider approaching a counsellor for professional help. After all, you want to make a sound, well thought out decision. Talk to someone who has gone through a separation, and with someone else who chose to remain in their relationship.

Examine your relationship closely:

What *real difficulties* do you have to live with at the moment, because of your partner's drinking? Write them down below.

What *benefits* do you get at the moment from your partner, despite his or her drinking? Write them down below.

In a few days time go back to these lists to see if there is anything you want to add or change.

Think about parting

What are you afraid will happen if you and your partner separate? Write down your fears.

What do you hope will happen if you choose to separate? Write down your hopes.

In a few days time go back to these lists as well to see
if there is anything you want to add, or change.

Ian eventually managed to talk to his girlfriend about
their relationship. She ended by saying she wasn't sure
how much she cared for him, because she felt mixed
up and confused about everything just then.

I put it to her that she'd never know what she
wanted out of anything until she stopped relying
so much on drink. She just refused to discuss it. I
ended up saying I didn't think there was any point
being together until she stopped or got some
advice. She said that was fine if it was what I

wanted. This hurt a lot, but I've talked it all through with my brother-in-law, and I'm now making plans to see a lawyer about separation. Then I'll talk again with her, and if her attitude is just the same I don't see any point in staying together. It's so hard because I still love her. I hope that after we're apart she'll think things over, and there'll be a change – but I have a lot of doubts.

Think again about staying together

In choosing to read this book, you have committed yourself to giving the relationship time and to accepting the problems for a while at least.

The questionnaire on page 140 helped you to pinpoint your problems. How severe are the problems that remain? How much time are you still willing to spend trying to improve things?

What do you owe your partner? What do your children deserve? What do you owe yourself?

These questions are not easy to answer. You will probably agonise about whether you can break up your family, and whether your partner will be able to cope alone. You may wonder if you can cope alone, and if you can bear to have a close relationship with anyone again. You *can*.

You can also seek help and advice. There are some excellent books to read on the subject of separation, and you can also get guidance from a marriage counsellor. Marriage counsellors help couples to separate as well as to stay together. Unmarried couples are also welcome to consult marriage counsellors about staying together or breaking up. You will find useful addresses to contact on page 160.

Preparing for separation

A counsellor and/or supporter can help you plan your separation (if you choose to separate) with an eye to limiting distress for all concerned. The main things to work out are:

- How to prepare the children for separation.
- Where to go for good legal and financial advice.
- Where to live if your partner refuses to leave. (See a solicitor to know your rights.)
- When to separate, since timing can be important.

Adjusting afterwards

It takes time to come to terms with all major changes, so you will need help to adjust after the separation and so will your children. After the initial relief, you may feel very guilty, and wonder if, after all, you aren't better off back together. Don't make important decisions without talking things over with someone you respect and trust. You will need time to settle down, and to learn to cope with things on your own. Even if you have handled your family's decisions and responsibilities alone for years, *being alone* is different and takes getting used to.

You may feel tempted to rush into *new* relationships – but beware of complicating rather than easing the effort of settling down again. The trick is to learn to balance and stand on your own feet, but don't expect too much of yourself too soon.

June separated from her husband after 12 years of marriage. Her husband had been hospitalised 3 times because of his drinking, but had never managed to stop for more than 2 weeks.

> It took a long time to get over my marriage breaking up, even though I didn't feel guilty about it because I knew I'd done everything possible to change the drinking. Five years later, I've built a new life, with a new home and a new job. I've been lucky because my children are now independent, and I had some help with money from my brother. The best thing that's happened is that I've got my confidence back.
>
> I know quite a few women who've steered their marriage through a drinking problem, and their relationships have come out stronger at the end of it all. This wasn't possible for me, but I know I've still got a lot of good things to look forward to in my life.

SUMMARY

You have taken stock of the progress you've made, and can now decide how to deal with the problems that still remain. You have also thought about your relationship with your partner, and are clearer about the sort of future you have to look forward to together. If, in the end, you feel you will have to make difficult decisions, get outside help as soon as you can. Excellent support and advice *are* available.

Hopefully, this book has helped with some of your problems and difficulties. Even if things haven't worked out as you hoped they would, try not to feel you have let yourself down. By having had the courage to face up to difficult problems in your life, you have learned a lot about yourself and other people. Most importantly, you have learned to believe in yourself.

USEFUL ADDRESSES

Additional sources of advice and information are mentioned in this book for those with severe problems which require extra help.

Your local alcohol agency is the most logical first source of help for you. The addresses of the national organisation to contact for information about local agencies are listed below.

ALCOHOL AND ADDICTION CENTRES

SCOTLAND
The Scottish Council on Alcohol
137–145 Sauchiehall Street
GLASGOW
G2 3EW

ENGLAND AND WALES
Alcohol Concern
275 Gray's Inn Road
LONDON
WC1X 8QF

NORTHERN IRELAND
Northern Council on Alcohol
40 Elmwood Avenue
BELFAST
BT9 6AZ

AUSTRALIA
The Alcohol & Drug Foundation Australia
GPO Box 477
CANBERRA
ACT 2601

NEW ZEALAND
Alcoholic Liquor Advisory Council
National Office
PO Box 5023
WELLINGTON

CANADA
Addiction Research Foundation
Russell Street
TORONTO 179

USA
NIAAA
5600 Fisher's Cane
ROCKVILLE
MARYLAND 20852

CHILD PROTECTION ORGANISATIONS

SCOTLAND
RSSPCC
Melville House
41 Polwarth Terrace
EDINBURGH
EH11 1NU

ENGLAND, WALES & NORTHERN IRELAND
NSPCC
42 Curtain Road
LONDON
EC2A 3NH

CANADA
CSPCC
356 First Street
Box 700
Midland
ONTARIO L4R 4P4

Family Violence Programme
Canadian Council on Social Development
55 Parkdale Avenue
PO Box 3505, Station C
OTTAWA
ONTARIO K1Y 4G1

USA

American Association for Protecting Children
The American Humane Association
9725 East Hampden Avenue
DENVER
COLORADO 80231–4919

SINGLE PARENT ORGANISATIONS

SCOTLAND

Gingerbread Scotland
304 Mary-Hill Road
GLASGOW
G20 7YE

ENGLAND

Gingerbread England
35 Watling Street
LONDON WC2

WALES

Gingerbread Wales
16 Albion Chambers
Cambrian Place
SWANSEA
SA1 1RN

NORTHERN IRELAND

Gingerbread Northern Ireland
169 University Street
BELFAST
B17 1HR

AUSTRALIA
Children's Services
66 Albion Street
Surreyhills
2010 NEW SOUTH WALES

NEW ZEALAND
Council for Single Mothers and their Children
63 Pansanby Road
AUCKLAND

CANADA
Parents Without Partners
205 Yonge Street
TORONTO
M5B 1NZ

USA
Parents Without Partners
International Headquarters
8807 Colesville Road
Silver Springs
MARYLAND 20910

CITIZENS/WELFARE RIGHTS ADVICE BUREAUX

SCOTLAND
Citizens Advice Scotland
26 George Square
EDINBURGH
EH8 9LD

ENGLAND & WALES
National Association of Citizens Advice Bureaux
115–123 Pentonville Road
LONDON
N1 9LZ

NORTHERN IRELAND
Northern Ireland Association of Citizens Advice Bureaux
Regional Office
11 Upper Crescent
BELFAST
BT9 5NW

AUSTRALIA
NZ Association of CAB
PO Box 9777
Courtney Place
WELLINGTON

**ORGANISATIONS PROVIDING ADVICE & COUN-
SELLING FOR PARTNERS**

SCOTLAND
Scottish Marriage Guidance Council
105 Hanover Street
EDINBURGH
EH2 1DJ

NORTHERN IRELAND, ENGLAND & WALES
Relate National Marriage Guidance Council
Herbert Gray College
Little Church Street
RUGBY
CV21 3AP

AUSTRALIA
National Marriage Guidance Council of Australia
Suite 8
696 High Street
East Kew
VICTORIA 3012

NEW ZEALAND
National Marriage Guidance Council of New Zealand
Private Bag
WELLINGTON

USA & CANADA
American Association for Marriage & Family Therapy
1717 K Street NW 407
WASHINGTON DC 20006

**ORGANISATIONS OFFERING ADVICE, SUPPORT
AND TEMPORARY ACCOMODATION FOR
WOMEN & CHILDERN AT RISK OF ABUSE**

SCOTLAND
Scottish Women's Aid
11 St Colme Street
EDINBURGH
EH3 6AG

ENGLAND & WALES
London Office
52 Featherstone Street
LONDON
EC1 8RT

FURTHER READING

Anxiety, Stress and Depression

Dr Clair Weekes, *Self-Help for Your Nerves*, Angus & Robertson

Peter Tyner, *How to Cope with Stress*, Sheldon, London

Relaxpack (Includes relaxation tape), Help Yourself Products, 181 Bruntsfield Place, Edinburgh EH10 5DG

Dorothy Rowe, *Depression*, Routledge

John Rush, *Beating Depression*, Century

K Nairne & G Smith, *Dealing with Depression*, The Women's Press

Tranquillisers

Trouble with Tranquillisers, Release Publications Ltd

Dr Valerie Curran & Dr Susan Golombok, *Bottling It Up*, Faber & Faber

Shirley Trickett, *Coming Off Tranquillisers*, SAT Publishing, Newcastle

Separation and Divorce

C. Shrieve, *Divorce: How to Cope Emotionally and Practically*, Turnstone Press, Wellingborough

J. Burgoyne, *Breaking Even: Divorce, Your Children and You*, Penguin

Anne Hooper, *Divorce and Your Children*, Unwin Paperbacks

Ginny NiCarthy, *Getting Free: A Handbook for Women in Abusive Relationships*, The Seal Press

Recovery from an Alcohol Problem

Scottish Council on Alcohol and Scottish Health Education Group, *The Road to Recovery*, available from Scottish Council on Alcohol

Scottish Health Education Group, *So You Want to Cut Down Your Drinking*, available from Scottish Council on Alcohol

INDEX

AA, *see* Alcoholics
  Anonymous
absences from work, 41
abuse: of children, 131–2; of
  partner, 3–4, 41, 87
accidents: BAC and, 28; at
  work, 41
activity list/diary, 18–19, 123
addicts, drinkers as, 36
Al-Anon, 70–1
alcohol, 20–33; and your
  behaviour, 23–4; in
  bloodstream, 25–8; and your
  body, 21–3; as drug, 21;
  finding out about, 136; in
  glass, 24–5; measuring
  drink, 24–8; safe drinking,
  28–9; units in drink, 26–8;
  what do you know about,
  31–3; your own drinking, 30
Alcoholics Anonymous (AA),
  16, 70–1
alcoholics, *see* problem
  drinkers
Alcohol Studies Centre, vii
anger, 3, 8, 15–17, 100, 134,
  135
anxiety: coping with, 78,
  102–6, 123; of drinker, 29;
  of partner, 8–10, 17, 140
apathy: of drinker, 41; fighting

against 99–100; of partner,
  76, 97
appetite, poor/loss of
  (partner's), 18, 97
arguments at home/work, 40,
  41
aspirin, 21
assault, 131–2

BAC, *see* Blood Alcohol
  Concentration
bad atmosphere at home, 40
bad feelings, 15–18 141, 144;
  of children, 135
Baillie, Pat, vii
beer, 23–4, 25, 26, 32
behaviour problems, 12–13,
  23–4, 41
Blood Alcohol Concentration
  (BAC), 27–8, 32
bloodstream, alcohol in, 25–8
Bradley, Mary, viii
breaking promises, 41
breastfeeding, 29
bruising, 40
burns, 40

changes, difficulties in making,
  140–2; coping with, 142–5
children, 46, 75, 121, 123,
  125–38, 140; feelings, 135;
  guidelines for, 134–8;
  helping them cope, 128–9;

needs, 127; preparing them for emergencies, 130–2; preparing them for separation, 152; what they can do, 136

cider, 26

Citizens Advice Bureau, 10, 87

coping: with drinking, 44–73; with difficulties, 142–5; with living, 74–124

counselling, 42, 43, 68, 69, 70, 71, 95, 105, 146, 152; see also marriage counsellors; supporters

covering up, 75

criticism of partner, unfair, 41, 93, 98, 100, 101

Cuthbert, John, vii

dangerous levels of drinking, 38

death, BAC and, 27

decision-making, 78, 107–8, 123, 140; stages in, 109–12

depressant, alcohol as 21

depression: dealing with, 78, 95–100, 123; of drinker, 29, 40; of partner, 4, 17–18, 140

diarrhoea, 40

disciplinary action at work, 41

dislike of workmates, 41

doctors (GPs), 77, 123, 131

domestic problems, 87–8, 140

drinkers, see problem drinkers

driving and drinking, 27–8, 32, 42–3, 95, 130

drug(s): 21, 77; alcohol as, 21

emergencies, preparing children for, 130–2

enjoyment, finding, 78–9, 123, 140; worksheet, 79–86

failure, sense of, 97

family: problems, 2, 75, 126, 134, 137; renewing contact

with, 91; as supporters, 93–4, 122

fears: of children, 126; of drinker, 12, 46–7 of partner, 3, 121–2, 123

financial advice, 152

fire, 131

food and alchohol, 23

forgetfulness, 41, 46

friends: breaking contact with, 45, 126; conflicts with neighbours and, 40; importance of, 89–91; making new, 91–2, 123; as supporters, 93–4, 122, 129; taking action as, 94–5; see also relationships

friendship list/diary, 96, 123

frustration of partner, 15–17

Glasgow Council on Alcohol, vii

group discussions, 70

guilt, 3, 100

health problems caused by drinking, 40

help, does your partner need it?, 42

helplessness, 3, 8, 97

holding back from people, 75–6

home, problems at, 40–1

hospitals, help from, 69–70

human body and alcohol, 21–3

illness, sudden, 130

impotence in men, 41

information sessions, 70

interest, loss of see apathy

irresponsibility, 45–6

irritability, 40, 126

jealousy, 41, 87

job hopping, 41

Lancaster, Ann, vii
large people and alcohol, 23
lateness for work, 41
learning to relax, 9
legal help, 120, 152
liver damager, 22, 40
loneliness: of children, 135; of
  partner, 3
losing heart, 141, 145
losing touch with people, 87–9

manipulation, of children, 131
marriage counsellors, 151–2
measuring how much you
  drink, 24
men and alcohol, 28, 31, 38
menstruation, 29
money worries, 40
mood changes, 41
moodiness, 40

nagging, 135
negative/positive thoughts,
  making list of, 14–15
night sweating, 40
nurses, 70

ovulation, 29

pain killers and alcohol, 21
panic attacks, 102
paranoia, 41
planning: to cope, 123–4; for
  future, 78, 118–19, 123, 140
police, problems with, 40
positive thinking, 9, 97, 99, 123
pregnant women, safety
  alcohol limits for, 28, 29
prescribed drugs and alcohol,
  21
problem drinkers: anxiety over
  8–10; behaviour towards
  partner, 12–13; and
  children, 46, 75, 121, 123,
  125–38; common types,
  34–7; coping, 44–73,
74–124, 142–5; denying
  problem, 46–8, detecting
  (for children), 134–5;
  drinking problems of
  partners, 30; emotional
  reactions caused by, 3–4, 8;
  facts about, 35; fathers as,
  127, 129, 131–2, 136; feeling
  useless about 10–11; future
  with, 145–53; if they decide
  to do something about it,
  66–9; how much they drink,
  37–8; men/husbands/
  boyfriends as, 2, 13–14, 22,
  35, 66–7, 69, 72–3, 78–9, 88,
  92, 98, 102, 105, 113, 141,
  146, 153; making sense of
  feelings about, 7–18;
  mocking approach of, 12–13;
  mothers as, 8, 77, 89, 125–6,
  136; reactions to (question-
  naires), 49–64; reasonable
  aims, 67–8; sons as, 47–8,
  90; taking action on
  (personal contract), 64–5;
  trying to survive effects,
  45–6; unhelpful changes,
  75–7; what help to expect,
  69–71; whether to
  compromise with, 68–9;
  women/wives/girlfriends as,
  4, 12–13, 25, 27, 42–3, 93–4,
  95, 107–8, 120, 143, 150–1
problems: caused by drinking,
  39–41; solving, 78, 108,
  113–14, 123, 140; solving
  exercises, 115–18
psychologists, 70

reactions to events, 101
rehabilitation centres, help
  from, 69–70
rejection, fear of, 98
relationships: building good,
  78, 79, 87, 91–2, 123, 140;

close examination of,
147–51; problems in, 41; *see
also* friends
relaxation, 9, 78, 104, 123;
exercise, 106
resentment: of children, 126;
of partner, 15–17
residential centres, private, 70
Royal College of Psychiatrists,
28

safe drinking, 28–9
SCA, *see* Scottish Council on
Alcohol
Scottish Council on Alcohol
(SCA), vii
seeking out drinking friends,
41
self-confidence, building, 139,
140
self-control and alcohol, 22
self-criticism, excessive, 98–9
self-help groups, 105
selfishness, 40
separation, *see* trial separation
sex, loss of interest in, 41
sexual abuse, 4; of children,
131–2
sleeping pills, 21, 77
sleeping problems, 40, 97
smoking, 77
social workers, 70, 105

spirits (whisky, gin, vodka),
23, 25
standing up for yourself, 100,
123, 140
stomach upsets, 40
stress, 78, 103–4
supporters, 93–4, 120, 123,
129, 140, 144, 146, 152

talking about problems, 137,
146; *see also* counselling;
supporters
tension, 102–4
tiredness, 40, 97, 98, 126
tolerance, alcoholic, 23
tranquillisers, 77, 105
trial separations, 119–21,
123–4, 145–6, 148–31

ulcers, 40
unconsciousness, BAC and, 27
unemployment, 16
uselessness, feelings of, 10–11

weight gain/loss, 24, 40, 98
well-being of partner, 13–15
wine, 24, 25
withdrawals, 69
women and alcohol, 28, 29, 31,
38
Women's Aid, 87
work, problems at, 41
worthlessness, 8, 11